John Pritchard is Bishop of 1
of England Board of Education. He was former p. of
Jarrow, Archdeacon of Canterbury and, before that, Warden of
Cranmer Hall, Durham. He has served in parishes in Birmingham
and Taunton, and has been Diocesan Youth Officer for Bath
and Wells diocese. Other books by the author include *The
Intercessions Handbook*, *The Second Intercessions Handbook*,
*Beginning Again*, *How to Pray*, *Living Easter through the Year*,
*How to Explain Your Faith*, *The Life and Work of a Priest*, *Going
to Church* and *Living Jesus*. He is married to Wendy and has
two married daughters.

D1458699

# GOD LOST AND FOUND

John Pritchard

First published in Great Britain in 2011

Society for Promoting Christian Knowledge
36 Causton Street
London SW1P 4ST
www.spckpublishing.co.uk

*British Library Cataloguing-in-Publication Data*
A catalogue record for this book is available from the British Library

ISBN 978–0–281–06352–9

1 3 5 7 9 10 8 6 4 2

Typeset by Graphicraft Ltd, Hong Kong
Printed in Great Britain by Ashford Colour Press

Produced on paper from sustainable forests

*For Wendy, who has faithfully accompanied me through the hills and valleys, and who first suggested this book*

# Contents

# A word at the beginning

When the American rock band R.E.M. released their song 'Losing my religion' they found they had a cult classic on their hands. As they put it, '"Losing my religion" feels like some kind of archetype that was floating around in space that we managed to lasso.' That might be absolutely right. There's a common human experience of losing touch with God and finding that faith is ebbing away. It's not deliberate. Few people set out to lose the reality of their faith, but somehow it happens.

When you scratch the surface of British churchgoing you're likely to find that many people are afraid to admit they no longer have a vivid experience of God. What was once bright and shiny is now tarnished and dull. What gave life and purpose has been reduced to disappointment and play-acting. We like to keep the mask on because it's so embarrassing to admit we no longer find any life in it. Nevertheless, some are bold enough to go public. They've tried; they've been round the course, but it just won't happen any more, if it ever did. The broadcaster John Humphrys writes, 'Along the way I have experienced the indoctrination of confirmation classes, the anticlimax of the eucharist, the futility of prayer, the contradiction between the promises made by an allegedly merciful, loving God and the reality of a suffering world. So I end up – so far, at any rate – as a doubter.'[1]

I once talked to a senior churchman who said he had been amazed at how many Christian people, later in life and themselves well-known figures, had quietly confided in him that they had lost the fire of their faith. When I'm preaching or leading a service I often wonder what it would be like if I could read the thought-bubbles above everyone's head. There would be faith, doubt, struggle, disagreement, anger: 'What on earth is this all about?' 'I've never experienced that.' 'What planet is he on?' But that's life. That's what people think and feel. There are no monochrome church congregations where everyone is a fully paid-up, passionate believer, with no hint of heresy or doubt. And some people are lonely behind the mask of hymn-singing and fellowship. It all used to be so vivid, but the colour has drained away. The ladder to the stars has been removed.

This book is about that experience, but also about where we might pick up the scent again, starting somewhere else, maybe somewhere completely different. The reasons for losing contact with God are multi-layered and complex, and they deserve to be named and understood. This in itself can be a relief to many Christians who feel guilty at their failure to be on fire with faith. I shall look at the way our inner spiritual experience of God can dry up, at how the failures of the church can leave us disillusioned with all religion, at how personal tragedy can destroy belief, and at how the secular assumptions of so much of society can be like acid eating away at faith. However, once these reasons have been understood and accepted there is much that can be explored as we try to put a reconstructed faith on a surer footing. This book is therefore 'a game of two halves', seeking to be realistic and honest in both.

Nothing is achieved by denying or minimizing the reality of this experience of losing touch with God. Continuing the foot-balling image, no one who has to play the full 90 minutes is going to avoid having periods of exhaustion and loss of con-centration. Anyone who tries to 'love the Lord your God with all your heart, and with all your soul, and with all your mind, and with all your strength' (Mark 12.30) is likely to have times of spiritual cramp.

The problem, of course, is that it's not like losing interest in stamp collecting or fly-fishing. The worst you have then is a cupboard full of stamps or a pile of fishing gear. With the loss of God may go an entire way of life – a framework of beliefs, values, practices and relationships that gave order, shape and meaning to our lives. It's even more difficult if you are a 'professional Christian', a priest, minister, or youth worker to whom many people look – perhaps a whole community. If you lose touch with God as a Christian leader, what do you do then? Most spiritual directors, at some time or other, have had the task of holding the broken pieces together. Imagine, for example, how innocent questions might expose a nagging doubt about vocation and faith in a situation such as is explored in Andrew O'Hagan's book *Be Near Me*. In this episode Father David has taken a group of wild youngsters to the island of Ailsa Craig:

Lisa stroked her shiny leg with a marigold and smacked her lips. She suddenly looked up at me as if she hadn't seen me before. 'Father,' she said, 'you have wasted your life, haven't you?'

'I don't think so,' I said. 'I believe in God. That has been my life.'

'It can't be,' she said. 'You could have been having a good time and you've wasted it.'

'That's not true, Lisa. Not from my point of view. We have different names for it, but I've lived according to my faith.'

'What is your name?'

'Sorry?'

'Your real name. What is it?'

'David Anderton.'

'So what's wrong with just being him?'

I stood up and spun a stone across the loch to make it jump.

'It must be quite boring,' she said, 'being Father somebody and having to go on like you're good all the time. Nobody else does. And then you end up here, in Bumblefuck, UK.'

'I am him,' I said, and I knew my voice was quiet. I was searching to say something permanent. 'Faith and good works,' I said. 'It's not *your* idea of a life, but it is mine.'

'Whatever,' she said. By that time the others had run over the verge and were panting beside us. 'He believes in God,' said Lisa, with a wide smile on her face.

'That's freaky,' said Mark. 'Him a priest as well.' . . .

We laughed and made our way over the rock and saw a cormorant rise from the reeds in the middle of the loch and fly off.

'He's a good laugh,' I heard Mark say behind me.

'He's wasted his life, though,' said Lisa.[2]

Father David may or may not have suspected that he had wasted his life, but it's not a good doubt to entertain, initially at any rate. It can cripple effective ministry, it can make familiar prayers die on the lips, it can reduce the heart to silence. Only later might a minister realize that the experience has led to a more honest and rewarding understanding of his or her vocation. What is true of a 'professional Christian' may also be true of others who apparently have less at stake, but in fact have just as much to lose existentially. Let's remember that Jesus was a layman, and he lost contact with his heavenly Father, catastrophically, one dark Friday we strangely call 'good'.

However, this shaking of the foundations need not be the end of the story. If the experience of loss can be named, understood and accepted there's much that can be done to put in train a process that reconstructs faith on a more secure footing. The experience of being betwixt and between, of being dislocated and outside our normal patterns of life and belief, can be profoundly creative. Indeed, these liminal spaces are usually the best places from which to grow. To raise the stakes still more, it could be said that too much religion is concerned with helping people to live comfortably within normal patterns of belief and practice. Cheap religion teaches people how to live successfully in a second-rate belief system and we end up wanting more and more of what doesn't really work. The explosive material of the gospel has been disarmed. The angels sigh.

So liminality can be good. Being displaced from our former certainties can open up possibilities and discoveries in the world of faith which are profoundly liberating and truth-telling. The journey starts again with new excitement. There are new pilgrims alongside us. The territory is strange but stimulating. And colour returns not just to our cheeks but also to the world around. Paradise regained. It's fascinating to learn in how many different ways the journey can get started and the blue touch paper can get lit. I knew an able woman who had been to church as a child but had put all that aside as she went through her teens, higher education, marriage and early family life. They moved house, and one Sunday morning she was hanging out the washing when she heard a single church bell not far away. The next day, as she drove her small son to school, she looked for the church to which that bell must have belonged. She found it, went next Sunday, and hasn't left it since. She's now ordained.

Our journey might deepen as a result of losing touch with God. It's a hard route to travel but it's a well-trodden path. This book is dedicated to those who have been there.

Thanks, as ever, go to Alison Barr, my editor who encourages and never fusses; to my wife Wendy who first said I should write this book and then went through it with a rigorous red pen; to Amanda, Christine and Debbie who kept the wider world at bay; to Veronica who read through the book and ironed out some of the more wayward infelicities; and to Whitby, our tortoiseshell cat, who in St Paul's words never lets me think more highly of myself than I ought to think.

My simple hope is that this book might help somebody who knows what it is to lose touch with the burning love of God and to sit by the embers, wondering what has happened. You might need to take a break and just sit awhile, but eventually it's worth trying again. Stand up, stir the fire, and throw on a new log.

# *Part 1*

# WHY?

# 1

## *When the well runs dry*

---

I sometimes ask a group I'm working with what season of the year they feel themselves to be in spiritually. Is it spring, with new growth budding in all sorts of places, tentative discoveries being made about God and a spiritual life that's well spiced with hope? Or is it high summer, with a spiritual life full of the presence and goodness of God in spite of the occasional storm of doubt? Or perhaps autumn is drawing on and some things that have been in flower are now dying away. There's still much green to enjoy and the grey weather has its own attraction, but nostalgia is in the air. Or maybe winter has well and truly arrived; the life of the spirit is pretty much dead and there are no signs of life. People tell us the potential is all there, just dormant and waiting to stir, but if we're honest we rather doubt this winter will ever end.

Most church life, most sermons and most popular Christian books assume a spring or summer spirituality. The truth, however, is that for many people of faith God has gone absent without leave, spiritual disciplines are wearying, prayer seems like talking to oneself, and to all intents and purposes they are living without God. And to make matters worse, they probably haven't told anyone about it and it's lonely.

In his last work the much-loved spiritual writer Henri Nouwen wrote:

> Do I like to pray? Do I want to pray? Do I spend time praying? Frankly, the answer is no to all three questions. After sixty-three years of life and thirty-eight years of

3

priesthood, my prayer seems as dead as a rock . . . The words 'darkness' and 'dryness' seem best to describe my prayer today . . .[1]

When this kind of experience swamps the spiritual batteries that for years have seemed so reliable, what's going on?

### *Bleak House*

*One of the reasons for this barren experience may be that we are simply overwhelmed with weariness on this Christian journey.* We've been on the road for a long time and have run into the sand. Changing the metaphor, the house of the Lord that seemed so full of light has become a bleak house, a place where we turn the handle of faith but it's become habit without reality.

The old monks used to call it *accidie*, meaning spiritual restlessness, boredom and an inability to concentrate. It can, however, affect anyone, because the truth is, rather obviously, that the Christian life is not all champagne and fireworks. As the spiritual writer Evelyn Underhill observed: 'A lot of the road to heaven has to be taken at 30mph.' Similarly, marriage isn't all romantic evenings and subtle seduction; it's also looking after a sick child in the night and remembering to take out the dustbin. What starts out as sheer magic has to settle into something deeper where the root systems of both lives have become so entwined that they simply know this commitment is for life.

Nevertheless, the spiritual restlessness we may feel is often part of a mid-life experience where many things are up for re-examination, from career and relationships to personal values and purpose. It can be a time of disillusionment or a sense of failure, of being trapped, of guilt and anxiety, of disconnectedness. It often goes with loneliness and a 'last chance' mentality. Many Christians feel deep down that they shouldn't be succumbing to any of this; didn't Jesus come to bring life

4

in abundance? Isn't the risen Christ our constant companion? 'Why are you cast down, O my soul?' (Ps. 42.5).

For the person of faith who has got used to seeing this relationship with God as being of ultimate importance, the loss of that original passion can cause not only lethargy but guilt and shame. The reality of God has ebbed away without the leak being noticed. I have a friend who was deeply involved in his church from childhood. It was his extended family. However, a personal crisis occurred and quite quickly he found that the receding tide of faith was exposing substantial rocks of doubt underneath, and nothing thereafter could cover them up. No spiritual experience tasted real any more, everything tasted of ashes and he felt he was letting everyone down – his church family (because he was going through the motions), himself (because he was covering up), and God (if he existed).

This experience of running out of spiritual fuel and drifting helplessly on to the hard shoulder is one to take very seriously. We can't run on empty for long. It affects most people some of the time, and some of the people most of the time. It's hard to admit and it's harder still to stop the slide. Going to church is meaningless except for the friendships. We find ourselves 'outside' the experience rather than inside. We critically examine everything that is said or done in the service because we are unable any more to give ourselves to worship with integrity. And so the dark clouds which were 'no bigger than a man's hand' become storm clouds filling the sky and blocking out the sun. Why read the Bible when it's so contradictory and, at times, downright unpleasant? Why pray when prayer bounces off the ceiling? There are better things to do than sit in a chair talking to myself. Bleak House indeed.

Sometimes the experience of emptiness is associated with overwork. One priest wrote this:

> They told me it was the best Christmas sermon they'd ever heard, but it certainly didn't feel like it at the time. I had

no idea what to say, and couldn't even face getting into the pulpit. I just drew up a chair and explained that I had no sermon, I felt helpless and empty with nothing to say. I don't know if I said any more than that – I can't remember. But afterwards people were making so many connections with the vulnerability and nakedness of Jesus, of God coming empty-handed with just himself, of stripping away the trappings of Christmas.[2]

What is particularly interesting about that reaction is that it demonstrates both how God can use our vulnerability when we often mistakenly think it's only our strength that matters, and also how vulnerability communicates to so many people because in fact it's a universal experience.

Losing contact with God is serious but it need not be fatal. It can give us a level of identification with others in this bleak place who together make up a fellowship of desolation, and it can also be another way of aligning ourselves with the God whose emptiness was a key dimension of his love. God emptied himself of his regal rights and entered his world from the 'underside'. Vulnerability is part of Christianity's basic script.

## Great Expectations

*Sometimes the well runs dry because we have great expectations of our spiritual journey and they turn out to be false.* There are three common variations on what is, in effect, a theology that has become skewed. The first is that God is far away and we have to try very hard if we are to find him. Such a view is understandable. The Old Testament in particular is very keen on emphasizing the 'otherness' of God in terms of both scale and character. The psalms are full of God's transcendence. 'The LORD is king, he is robed in majesty . . . he is girded with strength. He has established the world; it shall never be moved; your throne is established from of old; you are from everlasting'

(Ps. 93.1–2). To make matters better or worse, human beings cannot even understand this stupendous deity: 'For my thoughts are not your thoughts, nor are your ways my ways, says the LORD. For as the heavens are higher than the earth, so are my ways higher than your ways and my thoughts than your thoughts' (Isa. 55.8–9).

Two old monks are supposed to have made a pact that whoever died first would seek to convey to the other what heaven was really like. When one did eventually die he somehow managed to convey a message. What was it like? 'Totaliter aliter,' came the answer (predictably in Latin). It was totally other, he was saying, completely different from anything they could have conceived. But if God is so far removed from human experience what are the points of contact? When does transcendence become irrelevance?

The result can be that we might as well, to all intents and purposes, get on as if God were not around. God is getting on with his cosmic projects while we have to see to the school run. God is concerned about his own lofty thoughts while we have to pay the gas bill. If this is how remote God has become he can easily slip off the radar almost entirely. It could seem fairly futile to spend time in personal prayer when this Almighty God has such weighty matters on his plate. Why should he be bothered about Melissa's GCSEs? Before long the great and mighty Lord of whom the psalmist and the prophet Isaiah wrote has become so distant we end up in a form of functional atheism.

A second form of skewed theology is related. It's possible for some people to look for God only in spectacular experience and unusual events. God is present when people are healed, when there's a warm glow about the worship and all the spiritual lights are flashing. God is there when people are slain in the Spirit, or your heart is strangely warmed, or at the very least your little finger is twitching. The consequent search for the abnormal has been a severe burden on many people's

Christian journey. It has led to much disappointment and guilt as well as extraordinary feats of desire and lives of great courage, but that sense of personal spiritual failure has damaged many Christian lives, leading to unhealthy obsessions and too often the shipwreck of faith itself.

The sober truth is that the heavens are not always torn apart at 10.30 on a Sunday morning. Miracles don't come to order and many a person has gone home from a healing service baffled and disappointed. They had been led to believe that miracles would undoubtedly occur but no one seems much the better for two hours of exhortation to greater faith. The deeper question is always about the nature of the God to whom we are turning. What is our working model of how God relates to his world? Does God work from the outside, by pulleys and levers, or puppet strings, or advanced computer software? Or does God work from the inside, by loving persuasion and by stretching the potential of natural processes? If our model of God is too mechanistic we may find ourselves confused and hurt.

There's a milder version of this problem. We may not crave 'shock and awe' but we may still seek some more evidence of God's presence in our lives, something to give us more confidence that God is still around. I was in this place for a number of years. I used to mourn the lack of sensory support for the hours of prayer I offered and the sermons I preached urging confidence in the love of God for us all. Where was the experience of that love? Why did the curtain not twitch? How long can you believe in a love that you don't feel? I wrestled with this, prayed about it, read the right books and talked often with my spiritual director. I didn't ask for much but I did ask for something. What possible reason could God give for not answering a perfectly reasonable and modest request for a bit of first-hand experience? Just a touch on the emotional accelerator would have been fine. A new understanding dawned slowly, but that's for later in this book.

A third way in which our theology may be skewed is in a belief (quickly denied but often present) that God is – to put it crudely – 'out to get me'. The image of God that we subconsciously carry about with us needs careful exploration. How we imagine God will probably determine much of our Christian living, from the way we worship to the way we serve others, from the way we pray to the way we handle conflict and change. I have known a number of people whose picture of God has actually been that of a cosmic magistrate keeping a tally of our sins and virtues ('half marks and you're in'), or a celestial referee who's only too free with the yellow cards. They usually haven't recognized this fearful figure until asked to examine who God really is for them. Then they've realized why they have emotionally ducked when God has been mentioned; turning to their divine Father has actually been turning to their tyrant. Small wonder people lose contact with such a God. He's toxic.

The trouble with this image of God is that it's very subtle and insidious. The top level of our brain wouldn't remotely admit that God is anything other than benevolent, generous, merciful and kind. The lower level, however, may be working with quite a different model and this is where the operational understanding of God is located. I once knew an ordinand who was immensely gifted and was able to communicate persuasively about the gracious nature and eternal patience of God. Unfortunately he had another previously unrecognized picture of God who was not really to be trusted in the same way at all. God was like an inconsistent father who was fine when in public but whose behaviour at home was much less predictable. It wasn't so much that he was two-faced; just that he couldn't really be trusted to do what the student saw as the loving thing. God was inscrutable in this context and particularly bad at holding him through transitions. Perhaps, like this ordinand, we need to dig through the topsoil of belief and get into a deeper stratum of confidence in a God who doesn't guarantee

9

security and happy days, but guarantees instead that at rock bottom there is rock.

## *Hard Times*

The titles of Charles Dickens' novels continue to give us a handle on what might be causing the spiritual well to run dry. Here's a third reason. *There are Christians who hardly ever experience the reality of God's presence for large parts – even most – of their lives.* I once talked to an elderly nun who had been a faithful member of her community for over 60 years, praying the offices six times a day, and she admitted calmly that for all that time she had hardly ever experienced so much as a touch of God. Once, she said, just once, she had been overwhelmed by God's presence, but that was many years before.

Mother Teresa, by common consent, has been one of the saints of the last century but a book published after her death consisting mainly of letters between her and her confessors and superiors over 66 years reveals someone who for nearly half a century had felt virtually nothing of the presence of God. She wrote:

> When I try to raise my thoughts to heaven there is such convicting emptiness that those very thoughts return like sharp knives and hurt my very soul. I am told God loves me and yet the reality of darkness and coldness and emptiness is so great that nothing touches my soul. Did I make a mistake in surrendering so blindly to the Call of the Sacred Heart?

She wrote of her experience as 'the tunnel' and said: 'The more I want him the less I am wanted . . . such deep longing for God – repulsed, empty, no faith, no love, no zeal . . . pray for me please that I keep smiling at Him in spite of everything.'[3]

This is a hard place to occupy, year after year. Apart from the feeling of rejection there's the problem of inherent unfairness.

Why should one person be singled out for such poor treatment and not others? It doesn't much help to be told it's all in the mystery of God's will (a cop-out) or that we are specially favoured to be trusted with such emptiness (a decidedly back-handed compliment). How can that dear nun be expected to pray for 70 years while hardly ever experiencing a touch of spring in the winter of her soul? How miserable is that! The atheist has plenty of ammunition here for an assault on the entire scaffolding of belief. How does a God who never appears, never says anything, never gives a glimmer of response, never seems to wake up in answer to a million prayers, differ from no God at all? Answers on a postcard.

## *The sacred space in the dry well*

The well runs dry for many reasons. Because of weariness in the Bleak House of faith; because of theological misjudgements in our Great Expectations of God; because of Hard Times when we've been called, unwillingly, to the way of darkness and waiting. All these are reason enough to lose our early passion. The temptation might be to throw water down the well to try to fill it up again by ourselves, but this would be a mistake. The 'spring of water gushing up to eternal life' (John 4.14) has to come from Christ himself and not from our own panic.

Moreover, there can be real learning from these times of dryness. There are two primary routes to personal transformation and those are prayer and suffering. They both have the potential to take us to new places and to shift mountains of debris in our path. The suffering of unanswered prayer combines the two paths. Here then is a sacred space in which God may act in us at depth. Musicians are fond of saying that the space between the notes is as important as the notes themselves. In the dryness and the waiting we may become less arrogant and more humble, less certain and more searching, less selfish and more obedient.

Above all we may discover new things about the location of God. It is said that a thousand Indian children, Christian and Hindu, were asked to point to God. Almost all the Christian children pointed up to the sky; almost all the Hindu children pointed either to their own heart or to their neighbour's heart. God is not located far away, either theologically or spiritually. God is ever present, whether apprehended or not. When I was going through a bad period a friend gave me a poster. It said, 'Don't push the river; let it flow through you.' It was good advice. The point about real closeness is that you don't notice it. The point about good, healthy breathing is that you don't realize it's going on. God is never absent; he doesn't know how to vacate any part of his world. If we hang about long enough we might find that out for ourselves.

I shall attempt some answers to all these issues in Chapter 5. But for now let's live with the problem. It's real, and it's a lot more common than we might like to admit.

# 2

## *The Old Curiosity Shop*

One of the saddest reasons for people losing contact with God is that they've been involved with the Church but have become disillusioned. The Church which was supposed to be the Ideal Home Exhibition for Christianity turns out to be the weakest link. Some then turn away from the Church with a sigh of disappointment, some with genuine relief, some with deep anger. When the Church is attacked bishops and other leaders are often rolled out to defend the institution when the proper response might well be to agree and apologize. The Church fails day after day, but that's hardly surprising. It never claimed to be an Ideal Home, merely a home for seekers and finders, for the sick and the healthy, for honest pilgrims and honest doubters. It seems to be a kind of Old Curiosity Shop, full of strange and contradictory bric-à-brac. A friend of mine wrote:

> In two decades of parish life I really believed we Christians were keeping the spiritual banner aloft in a materialistic Britain. But I found in X [place deleted to protect the innocent] that many people thought we had fallen down on the job and that the task of being God's people was being handed over to others. Christians were seen as Bad News; a suppressed anger was directed at the churches, and Christianity was seen as turning aside to worship the gods of this present world – power and finance. The caricature of churches as hopelessly weak or spiritually sterile had sunk deep. Almost universal was an indignation that too

many Christians declare themselves right and all others less right or downright misguided, whilst offering a narrowed down vision of the Divine.

What has gone wrong?

## *Damaging experience*

The truth is that people can get damaged by the Church. Sometimes they are overworked, sometimes undervalued, sometimes bullied. Sometimes their good will is abused; sometimes they are manipulated and made to feel guilty; sometimes they are taught in damaging ways. Sometimes they are badly let down by the leadership; sometimes they are caught up in arguments and ways of behaving that wouldn't be acceptable in secular settings, let alone the household of God. It's all very wounding and it's no surprise that the victims don't want to return to the scene of the crime.

It can too easily be the case that a church doesn't offer an experience of authentic relationship. There can be denial that anything is amiss, rejection of difference, fear of intimacy, an unwillingness to face problems and a superficiality of relationship that means people bounce off one another without ever really encountering each other's depth and complexity. For example, I have a friend who is often moved to tears by her faith but she says she only knows one church where she is safe to cry without the likelihood of whispers and premature counselling. Relationship is the core operation of the Church and if it fails there it fails everywhere.

A different kind of damage can be done to churchwardens who may find themselves handling paperwork from the diocese, overseeing repairs to the church building, controlling the whole 'front of house' experience of worship on Sundays, going to endless meetings, and trying to keep the overworked vicar from a nervous breakdown. If there is conflict they will inevitably find themselves caught in the midst of it, and if members of the congregation have problems with what's going on in the life of the church they will be left with impossible dilemmas of confidentiality, support and problem solving. Rather than throw in the towel I hope such a person may be able to change the way he or she operates in that post. In extreme cases, however, it may be best to stand down – personal faith should not be the casualty of someone generously taking an office in the church. I was once talking to a church treasurer who said he'd occupied that role for 52 years. 'That's wonderful,' I replied encouragingly. 'It's madness,' he shot back.

There is a deeper worry here, however, and that is that the faith being proclaimed and lived in a particular church may itself be genuinely unhealthy. I often long for Christians to have a faith that's a kind of 'extreme discipleship', akin to young people's fascination with extreme sports. Young people usually want something solid to crunch on, not the soft pap they are often offered. However, the other side of that strength of commitment may be a toxic and unhealthy extremism.

In his book *Between the Monster and the Saint* Richard Holloway writes about the well-known story of Abraham taking his son Isaac up the mountain to sacrifice him as he believes the Lord is calling him to do:

As Abraham hung over him, about to cut his throat, Isaac must have realised that he lived in a dangerous and unpredictable universe in which a son might be sacrificed to the demands of a voice in his father's head that was more powerful than any human love. To put it another way, you can't trust a believer, even if he is your father. That is the devastating insight that makes the secular mind anxious about the unpredictable power religion has to plunge people into evil madness. How can you negotiate the intricacies of living alongside people who are programmed by an invisible, inaudible voice?[1]

Unthinking interpretations of the Bible can lead to all sorts of misunderstandings. The Old Testament contains many passages that could lure the unsuspecting reader into pictures of God as a bloodthirsty tyrant. It has to be made clear that, although the Bible has a superb narrative unity in its overall theme of the saving love of God, it is the product of many minds and motives over some fifteen or more centuries and it reflects an evolving understanding of the nature of God. There are flashes of gold but equally some dire passages of prejudice and spite. The interpretative principle is always the character of Jesus Christ; does this passage fit with the picture of God that we have in Jesus? But some Christians persist in reading off their interpretations verse by verse, irrespective of context. American conservatives who would bring on a nuclear or environmental apocalypse to hasten the fulfilment of the book of Revelation are a dangerous breed. There are Christian Zionists who want the Palestinians driven out of the Holy Land to fulfil their reading of the promises of Exodus. That too is irresponsible politics and terrible hermeneutics. Through the centuries, Christians have been implicated in the persecution of both black and gay people on the basis of their reading of Scripture.

The examples of unhealthy religion multiply. An angry God who has to beat up his own son to appease his own sense of justice is an image that has lodged in the minds of many a Christian who has subsequently abandoned ship. I have been told (mistakenly!) by students of mine that pastoral care is effected mainly from the pulpit and that no one can pray until they have come to a personal faith in Jesus Christ. (What do the other hundreds of millions of praying people think they are doing, I wonder?) People with psychiatric illness are given heavy-duty deliverance ministry which only makes their distress worse. Far too many priests have been guilty of the outrageous crime of child abuse, and some have been protected by their superiors. People are taught that the more faith they have the more financial rewards they will achieve – a success gospel that

looks tawdry when set alongside the image of a man hanging
on a cross for love of the world. But this is what religion can
look like when it becomes unhealthy. It can appear demanding
and repressive, far removed from the freedom-giving faith of
Jesus. Small wonder that some people lose sight of the burning
beauty of a God whose love for them is unconditional and
utterly reckless. He has been lost in a black forest of unpleasant
motives and destructive activities.

The author Louis de Bernières wrote:

> I am longing for the day when Bishops resign en masse
> as a protest against the feckless master they have served
> so long, with so much misplaced trust. Humans, at least,
> are capable of nobility and altruism, and this makes us
> morally superior to God, who would appear to be like
> an Ottoman sultan. He is an absolute despot who is out
> of control of his empire, surrounded by sycophants,
> answerable to no-one, drunk with apathy, who demands
> homage and taxes from his people without offering any
> services in return.[2]

The writer's anger shows through. Sometimes I can understand
why.

As with all human ideologies and institutions, fallibility is
written into the fabric of religion, and like all deep instincts it
can be twisted into a distorted parody of itself. As with all dis-
tortions, the original instinct is good and true, but when any
instinct is twisted far enough it can descend into a nightmare.
Love can degenerate into lust and abuse, friendship can become
possessiveness, eating can become gluttony, social drinking
can become violent mayhem – and religious faith can become
fanatical prejudice. The instinct itself isn't wrong; the problem
comes in the twisting. As John Saxbee put it, 'If religion is charac-
terised by the recruitment of God to serve our agendas, and faith
is about putting our agendas at the service of God, then clearly
there is too much religion in the world and not enough faith.'[3]

## Black boredom

When I was a diocesan youth officer I remember a report coming out on young people and the Church. There was a particularly vivid image given by a young person who was asked what he thought of church services. He said they were utterly boring, 'like drinking ten cups of tea one after the other'. There must be some basis for the story of the apocryphal child who, as the service droned on, whispered in anguished tones to his mother, 'Mummy, is it still Sunday?' Indeed most of us, on some occasion in a church service, have probably been close to losing the will to live.

One problem of course is that we live in a culture where every public presentation of any sort is likely to be judged by its entertainment value. Worship rightly resists that benchmark but this expectation does at least mean that those who prepare and lead worship know they have to work to high standards. Quality matters, whether it be in music, preaching, public prayer, the drama of the Eucharist, the atmosphere, pace and imagination of the worship, the lighting, visual stimuli and symbols, and even the welcome, the seating and the quality of coffee. Above all, those responsible for worship are there to help people see beyond the here and now to the luminous presence of another reality which interpenetrates our own at every point. Worship that has no sense of the beyond in our midst and no sense of mystery is likely to leave people feeling encouraged by the refreshing of friendships but unfulfilled at that level of the spiritual ache which is a major element of the human condition.

Whatever else we say about God, he surely cannot be boring. The God of the constellations, of the Himalayas and the horny backed toad, the inspiration behind Bach's B minor Mass, Michelangelo's Pietà and Durham cathedral – this God must be overwhelmingly colourful, creative and joyful. Worship should celebrate the magnificent otherness and intimacy of God, not be a way of passing an hour on a Sunday morning if you have nothing better to do. Better that a faith should go down in flames than that it should simply dry up.

## A reactionary community?

Some people stumble in their faith not because of the boredom of the worship but because of the perceived reactionary nature of the institution itself. The Church seems to change by reluctant inches rather than – as in other parts of life – by leaps and bounds. There is a deep seduction in the Church that leaves people wanting to keep the barns warm and well painted even if God's harvest is rotting in the fields. Sometimes it can seem as if the Church is a wagon with square wheels, carrying a load of round wheels, but insisting that using the square wheels is much more honouring to God. There is an answer . . .

The Church today is in danger of being left on the wrong side of history. It appears to be obsessed with sex and gender issues and with protecting its back, and this is making it increasingly irrelevant and incredible to a society facing really important questions about war, global terrorism, the environment, poverty, failed states, economic instability, corruption, HIV & AIDS and a whole lot more. Faced with this tsunami of issues, the Church can seem to be preoccupied with building sandcastles on the beach – and destroying those of their brothers and sisters whose castles dare to be different.

The popular American author Anne Rice returned to her Christian faith in 1998 but announced on Facebook in 2010 that she was stopping being a Christian – in the name of Christ. She said:

> In the name of Christ, I refuse to be anti-gay. I refuse to be anti-feminist. I refuse to be anti-artificial birth control. I refuse to be anti-Democratic. I refuse to be anti-secular humanism. I refuse to be anti-science. I refuse to be anti-life . . . When does a word (Christian) become unusable?

When does it become so burdened with history and horror that it cannot be evoked without destructive controversy? . . . It's simply impossible for me to belong to this quarrelsome, hostile, disputatious, and deservedly infamous group. For ten years I've tried. I've failed.

And yet she said that her faith in Christ is central to her life.

My conversion from a pessimistic atheist lost in a world I didn't understand to an optimistic believer in a universe created and sustained by a loving God is crucial to me. But following Christ does not mean following his followers. Christ is infinitely more important than Christianity and always will be, no matter what Christianity is, has been, or might become.[4]

I suspect there are many people who will echo these hard sayings. A thoughtful young person who wants to take his or her global citizenship seriously could be forgiven for thinking that the Church just isn't the place to start.

## *The sea of grey hair*

This takes us to another way in which the Old Curiosity Shop may disappoint those who want to encounter a living faith. I am no one to talk since my hair is a distant memory, but it remains true that, when I look out on very many church congregations on a Sunday morning from the vantage point of the pulpit, I often find I'm looking out on to a sea of grey hair. There are sparkling exceptions where it's difficult to find such a noble mane and young families are pouring into church, but the problem of an ageing church is well known. (Not, of course, around the world because the average Christian in most parts of the globe is young, coloured and female.) The average age of an Anglican churchgoer in Britain now is 61, and 48 per cent of churchgoers are over 65. Young families tend to cluster in churches that have made a particular effort to accommodate their needs. If you are under 50 in Britain today you may well feel that the Church is not for you, and you will almost certainly feel that it isn't at the cutting edge of very much that interests you.

There's another age factor in play as well. The churches in Britain have weekly contact with a million children in church schools, but what happens to them when they move to secondary school is typically that they stop any church-related activity because no one else among their friends has any such contact. Peer pressure is strong. The faith that may have been growing in them through primary school and church groups then withers for lack of nourishment. The sense of wonder, spiritual exploration and openness to mystery, story and symbol dries up, to be replaced by a flood of new experiences through a variety of screens and gadgets – digital HD television, computers, mobile phones, games, iPods, iPads and the next big thing.

Many young people will never look to the Church to satisfy any of the spiritual questions they will almost certainly have in the years ahead.

## A Church that isn't different enough

Some people are disappointed with the Church because its interests and ways of working simply aren't different enough from the preoccupations and obsessions of the rest of society. The Church can seem to be like any other mildly dysfunctional club with its own rules, its own opinion formers and its own barrack-room lawyers. The only difference is that its leisure interest of choice is religion. Moreover, the faith that it speaks about just isn't interesting enough. It doesn't seem to be dealing with big ideas and far-reaching visions of society, but rather with the muddle of middle-class organizational life – harvest suppers, building repairs, accounts, elections and reports from sub-committees. Where is the faith that changes the world? Where is the prophetic word that shakes society? Where is the faith that provokes, inspires, stimulates, and keeps you awake at night, thinking?

If a church is timid and anxious it means, according to Alison Morgan, that

> insofar as we do engage with the world our contribution is mostly a worried attempt to restrain it; afraid for our children, we strive to uphold the moral standards of a sliding culture by campaigning against abortion or disapproving of stories about wizards. The result is that we keep our moral and spiritual integrity but our witness is lost.[5]

This isn't an agenda to set the pulses racing and therefore large numbers of spiritual seekers and thoughtful citizens never encounter the radical, life-changing gospel for which countless Christians have given their lives.

Michael Frost in his book *Exiles* retells a parable by the Christian philosopher Søren Kierkegaard:

> Noticing that a flock of wild geese had settled on his property on their long flight home for the winter, Kierkegaard was intrigued when they didn't fly on as the weather turned colder. In fact, this flock sheltered in his yard and waited out a relatively mild winter on his pond. At first, the Danish philosopher was delighted to have his own resident family of geese. Then he was disturbed to notice how with the onset of each subsequent winter, as other wild geese flew south, his geese would rankle and squawk and fuss among themselves. The honk of the wild geese flying overhead awakened within his geese some primeval urge to fly, but they never did. Some flapped their big wings and took to the air briefly, but they returned and enjoyed the safety of Kierkegaard's farm. Then came a winter when the honking geese overhead raised no reaction at all from the land-bound flock. They pecked at the earth, oblivious to the call of the wild overhead.

Michael Frost goes on:

> [That] might well describe the Western church today. Some
> churches still hear the wild honking, and their feathers will
> bristle, their heart will skip a beat, their lungs fill with air
> ready for the long flight ahead of them. But their feet don't
> leave the ground. They love to read about the Christian
> heroes who have forged new movements, addressed grand
> plans, planted new churches, fed the hungry, fought for
> justice, but they prefer the security of the farm.[6]

A faith founded on the extraordinary life of Jesus ought to stir
hearts to their core. Jesus is the centre point of history, and the
story of his life, death and new life has been the most formative
narrative the world has known. That we should make it a safe
domestic tale without danger or passion is the final indignity
and the Church must take responsibility. But let's be sure to
blame the singer, not the song.

Essentially what the Church often misses is the transformative effect of a mission agenda. In his book *The Ritual Process*,[7]
the anthropologist Victor Turner draws a distinction between
community and *communitas*. Community is the agglomeration
of individuals who meet together around a particular interest.
This interest can be as mundane (or exciting, depending on your
passion!) as stamp collecting or pre-war London buses, but the
internal dynamic is about the maintenance of the group and
the satisfaction of the individuals who make it up. *Communitas*,
on the other hand, is the experience of people who engage
in a common task outside their own satisfactions. It's a happy
spin-off, a serendipitous by-product of a larger task, and it
comes in the experience of liminality, of standing outside the
cosy community. In Christian terms *communitas* comes about
not by a church setting up a programme to achieve that goal
as an end in itself, but by a group of Christians finding an
inspiring purpose and pursuing it in the power of the Spirit.
Trying to be a community of happy, shining Christians won't

achieve anything except the normal power plays and conflicts of human groups left to themselves. On the other hand, *communitas* emerges naturally when a church commits itself to honesty and to a mission beyond itself. That, sadly, is why people sometimes say that they have more of an experience of fellowship in a drama group or a sports team than in their church. I once knew a priest who said the same about his Alcoholics Anonymous group as well.

I have often thought that if a church thinks it has all the answers then it isn't asking big enough questions. The world is asking big questions; our churches need to be part of the exploration of both the big questions and the big answers. One way of describing the problem is to say that the Bride of Christ spends too long looking in the mirror.

## The Church isn't spiritual enough

I've saved the most damning critique until last. If a church isn't spiritual enough it has surely fallen at the first fence. If the church isn't passionate about God why should anyone else be bothered? If God isn't our magnificent preoccupation the world might wonder why we exist at all. I have a suspicion that some church life nudges God out of the way as the prime object of commitment for some churchgoers. It's what happens in church and who's doing what, when and to whom that they talk about, rather than what might be going on in God and what God is doing, when and to whom. The spiritual seeker might well be disappointed if he or she listened in to the coffee conversations after the service on Sunday or the church council discussion during the week.

Some research conducted by Willow Creek, the seeker-friendly church in Chicago, highlights the issue rather painfully. This research project used thousands of questionnaires as well as in-depth interviews to find out about people's spiritual journeys and what moved them most deeply. The definition they used for spiritual growth was, 'An increasing love for God and other people', based on the two aspects of Jesus' great commandment. From the responses, they found that people could be seen as belonging to four distinct groups – those exploring Christianity, those growing in Christ, those close to Christ and those who were Christ-centred. They also found that the church is most important in the early stages of spiritual growth, but its role thereafter shifts to one of secondary importance.

The results then get more challenging. More than 25 per cent of those surveyed described themselves as spiritually 'stalled' or 'dissatisfied' with the role of the church in their spiritual growth, with those who were 'Christ-centred' providing most of the 'dissatisfied'. This latter group certainly attended services regularly, participated in small groups, often volunteered, and were more diligent than others in reading the Bible and praying, but *63 per cent of them were considering leaving the church because they were dissatisfied and were looking for more depth from every aspect of church life.* They wanted the church to challenge them to greater spiritual maturity and to hold them accountable. (Twenty-five per cent of those defined as 'close to Christ' were also considering leaving.)[8]

These are telling statistics. How spiritual is the Church? Does the Church infantilize people and give prescriptive guidance on how to live properly and conventionally? The danger may be that we leave thoughtful, sensitive people perpetually in the shallow end of the spiritual swimming pool when they long to strike out to sea. In the Christian life it's a dangerous heresy to think we have 'arrived'. The image of the journey or the pilgrimage is much more fruitful. Richard Giles, a former dean, says:

In a contemporary culture where individuals in pursuit of success spend so much of their time giving you the impression that they have 'arrived', it is a beautiful thing that the Church should exult in its conviction that we are a community that never arrives . . . This conviction that the community of faith is always on a journey is a refreshing tonic to a jaded world . . . The whole Judaeo-Christian story is a travellers' tale. Moreover, it is a cautionary tale which warns that coming to a halt, settling down and building bigger barns is usually a sign that decline and fall is imminent.[9]

A sense of being on a quest is part of this model of pilgrimage. We can never have the Christian faith caught in a jar and put on a shelf. It must remain an exploration until the end of our lives. My father was a good parish priest who had given his whole life to ministry. He once told me that when he was ordained he had decided he wanted his theology all sorted out by the age of 27 and then all his pastoral skills honed by the age of 30. In his late seventies he was still buying learned commentaries with Greek translations! The journey is lifelong and all the richer for the constant fascination of an ever-deepening exploration.

It's interesting to note that the way Jesus engaged people spiritually was not usually with an *ex cathedra* statement but very often with a question. 'What do you want me to do for you?' he asked blind Bartimaeus in Jericho (Mark 10.51). 'Do you want to be made well?' he asked the paralysed man at the pool of Bethesda (John 5.6). 'Who do you say that I am?' was the direct question he put to the disciples at Caesarea Philippi (Matt. 16.15). 'Which of these three was a neighbour to the man who fell into the hands of the robbers?' he asked, after telling the parable of the Good Samaritan (Luke 10.36). And note the first things that the risen Jesus said to his bewildered followers: 'Woman, why are you weeping?' (John 20.13), and to the disciples wending their way disconsolately to Emmaus, 'What are you discussing with each other while you walk along?' (Luke 24.17). Jesus wants to engage people at their point of real concern, and he does this by asking them to articulate their need. Is that not a better way for the Church than proclaiming dogmatic truths from a great height? The historian Diarmaid

MacCulloch wrote a piece in *The Guardian* addressed to the Archbishop of Canterbury. It ended:

> You will know the saying of Thomas Aquinas which a wise old Dominican friar once quoted to me over a great deal of Irish whiskey, that God is not the answer, he is the question. As long as your church and all other churches go on asking the question, they will never die.[10]

A genuine spirituality for the contemporary Church may well be one that opens up questions on a continuing journey of faith. It may also be one that is more humble in what it thinks church services can deliver. For example, is it necessary to expect that the presence of God should be a felt experience for everyone at every service?

Research for a doctorate once revealed that of all those people emerging from church services on a particular Sunday morning in Wolverhampton, only 5 per cent reported that they felt they had had any direct experience of God in that worship. Perhaps a better approach would be that of Shug Avery, one of the unlikely heroes of Alice Walker's book *The Color Purple*. She says to her friend:

> Celie, tell the truth, have you ever found God in church? I never did. I just found a bunch of folk hoping for him to show. Any God I ever felt in church I brought in with me. And I think all the other folks did too. They come to church to share God, not find God.[11]

If the Church is to be the place of spiritual resource that most people expect it to be, it will have to modify its practices and be more overtly intrigued by the question of God and more passionate about the importance of spirituality. It will have to demonstrate that holy fascination by the priority it puts on prayer, on imaginative spiritual exploration and on the pursuit of depth. Without these priorities the Church may simply be chatting to itself on the comfortable way to functional oblivion.

# 3

## *The tragic facts of life*

She was just eighteen months old and living was a bubbly adventure. She raced around with a look of delighted concentration on her face, her whole body alive with the amazing new possibilities of moving from one place to another. Occasionally she would arrive at the knees of an adult – any adult would do, known or unknown – and fling her arms in the air to be picked up, so she could celebrate life with someone else.

And then she fell over. Immediately her body crumpled and her face registered the surprise of finding herself on the floor. 'How did that happen?' it seemed to ask. Then came the tears, more of indignation than of pain. The face creased up; cheeks were wet; loud noises were emitted. But it was soon over. It's amazing what a cuddle can do to put the world right. She went back to the serious business of racing around.

Toddlers give us a picture, in an extreme form, of what we are all like both when times are glorious and when times are hard. We are a unity of body, mind, spirit and context, and if one part of us is hurting, other parts of us will react in sympathy (St Paul said the same thing: see later). So it's the tragic facts of life that often damage our awareness of God's presence. Things happen to us that are unpredictable and damaging, and our bewildered mind is often reflected in a bewildered spirit. When asked by a journalist what was most likely to blow a government off course, the former Prime Minister Harold Macmillan replied, 'Events, dear boy, events.' It's the same in other spheres of life. What's most likely to throw our spiritual life off course? Events, I'm afraid, events.

## Personal facts of life

Just like that toddler, when life comes up and hits us, figuratively we curl up in a ball. It can happen through the loss of a loved one. A friend had just lost his mother. He was about to go to theological college to train to be an Anglican priest but he was affected by this loss at a deeper level than he had ever imagined. He lost confidence in himself, in his calling and even – though he didn't want to face this – in God. He was an intelligent person and could rationalize what was going on, but the effect was the same. Where had the clear flightpath gone? Where was the Pilot?

It happens with illness. Even sophisticated believers can lose their balance when faced with serious ill health. The body which has hitherto been a safe vehicle through life has shown itself to be vulnerable and unreliable. Worse, the reassuring concepts, the comforting prayer, the measured beliefs by which we have lived, have been shaken by this unexpected intruder. The bleak mental landscape doesn't respond to intelligent reasoning. And God maintains radio silence. Even a lifetime of faithful believing is shaken when we can no longer say that 'all things work together for good', and when the Lord no longer 'makes me lie down in green pastures' or 'restores my soul'.

Depression, in particular, can strip our sense of self-worth as we slide into the long velvet darkness known by so many people. A friend wrote of his helplessness as he sensed daylight fleeing and 'hordes of demons swarming back gleefully'. The writer Justine Picardie wrote in *The Times*, 'It was a black tangle of misery, anxiety, rage, grief, terror, panic, loss, jumbled up into a churning state of overwhelming unhappiness.'[1] It's a bare, featureless country suffering prolonged drought and an alarming absence of road signs.

Another friend said it was like this when depression overwhelmed her:

When the universe is shuttered and silent, when the light appears to have been extinguished and one finds oneself trapped in darkness and emptiness, the worst fears – real and imagined – emerge. The heart gives up its (unknown) secrets – secret rage, secret jealousies and envies, secret fear, self hatred – and mixed in are feelings of nothingness, meaninglessness and worthlessness. Do I matter? Do I count? Does anyone care? The questions seem only to reverberate, unheard. The lack of response is deafening. The noise of one's pain drowns out any answer or holding that might be offered. Rigid defendedness doesn't allow relaxing into the hold of God.

For a believer, the lack of response from God is the hardest cut. But it's an experience that has been shared before we ever get there. As that friend went on to say, 'Where can one go in dereliction except to the foot of the cross?' Jesus found that the silence of heaven didn't stop him calling out into the deserted space, putting the question for all humankind, 'Why?' Why have you forsaken me at my lowest point?

Stress can have a similar, if shorter and less dramatic, effect. I remember that in my own brush with nervous exhaustion I no longer had any awareness of God just when I needed him, and had to rely (gladly) on the prayers and love of others, who mediated God's care to me. I had come to the end of my resources, expending every ounce of personal energy on a particular project until my battery was completely flat and my body sent out alarm signals in all directions. I needed the wise ministrations of a Christian doctor to explain what was happening and to get me to build up the reservoir of energy with large quantities of rest, but I found it alarming not to have any live contact with my spiritual HQ. All the lines were dead.

Accident is one of the most shocking interruptions to the easy assumptions of our lives, and it puts faith into very rough

water. The former poet laureate Andrew Motion had a conventional Christian upbringing and went to a school with
a distinctive religious foundation, but then his mother had a
calamitous riding accident. He said of his school:

> It had a very clear religious structure, chapel every day,
> more extended worship on Sundays, and I was very inter-
> ested in this. Sometimes I used to go more than once a
> day, in that swooning, obsessive way that adolescents can
> have. Then almost immediately after my mother's accident,
> I started to walk away from it. I thought, this is crazily
> unfair and a betrayal of all the things I have believed in.
> I lost my faith in about a week, and at the end of the week
> I thought well, what was all that about?[2]

Disaster can also be experienced vicariously. A friend wrote:

> I lost God when I was angry with him and put up a big
> wall in my mind to keep him out. A young friend had
> been diagnosed with a serious illness he would have for
> the rest of his life. Bravely he accepted that, and got on
> with his new life. But the breaking point came when his
> lovely young wife had a miscarriage after they had been
> waiting a long time for a baby. Both were fine Christian
> people, and it seemed so unfair that this should happen
> to them. Why should I let God in when I was so cross
> with him on their behalf?

These personal facts of life can send a believer in one of two
directions. They can take us further into the secure reality of
God or they can drive us away. No one can tell which way they
or others will respond when ill chance comes knocking. I
once took a service for people who had been bereaved following road traffic accidents. No congregation could have been
more focused. These were people who had paid the highest
price imaginable for humanity to have the internal combustion
engine. The evil day would have dawned like any other, with

a rush round the kitchen, a quick goodbye, a slam of the door. And that was the end. Never again. Full stop. End of sentence. So this congregation was serious. Somehow they had come to a point where they could bring themselves to this service and place all this pain before God. It was a move in one of the two directions.

On the other hand, there would be many who wouldn't come to such a service because the nails in their loved one's coffin were also nails in the coffin of their faith. Either God was callous, arbitrary and not to be trusted, or tragedy had finally erased him from their minds and hearts as non-existent. Dostoevsky has one of his characters say, 'Can't I simply be devoured, without being expected to praise what devours me?'[3] It's an understandable reaction. On the other hand, there are many who say, 'Can't we simply accept that God doesn't exist?'

However, for those who dare to trust that God is still good, some part of the mental furniture may have to move. The magician version of God, who keeps us all safe if we pray or if we're good, will have to be deposited in the attic of lost dreams. After personal loss and tragedy I have often heard people say some variation on the words, 'There must have been a reason,' or, 'God's ways are not our ways.' But this won't do. We can't retreat into religious obscurantism. We need some understanding of God and the world that allows for disaster without crumbling into blind fatalism. We could at least begin with the conviction that love cannot be coercive. It has to allow for chance and accident; it has to be possible for love to be rejected. If this world is to have real value, it has to have a truly radical freedom, and God has to tie one hand behind his back and submit to the limitations of a finite creation. And this limitation applies to the physical world as well as the world of human interaction. The possibility of movement in the earth's crust is as necessary as the possibility of movement in a lover's heart.

Bishop John V. Taylor said:

I no longer think of God as a super chess-player who, if only
he will, can move any of the pieces around and win the
game. . . . I think that God is engaged in a much longer
and more dangerous adventure in which there is a great
deal of accident around: that's the sort of world that God
has made and allowed and has submitted himself to.[4]

God does all that love can do, but there are limits to what even
love can do in a world that, once created, has its own regularities
and patterns. God remains eternally active but God's way of
working is to 'underrule' rather than 'overrule' his creation. That
radical, costly freedom is too valuable to undermine, but this
way of thinking may require a lot of thinking through.

And yet the divine imperative is impossible for many to ignore.
The young film-maker Samantha Morton spent years in and out
of care and foster homes. Along the way she experienced such
violence, sexual abuse and torture that she had to dilute it for
the film she made which drew on that upbringing (*The Unloved*).
She said she didn't want to make a 'horror film'. However, she
said that she could not have survived without her faith.

I suppose what I'm trying to say is that I felt watched
over as a kid [and I still feel it]. I'm not a Bible thumper,
but I have a wonderful joy in my life, and that is that
I have always believed in God. I just have and I think I'm
lucky . . . it's what got me through it all.[5]

For the time being, however, let us simply note that personal
tragedy is also the cause of much spiritual confusion and loss.
God seems to go silent; the lines are down. Many who are
reading this will know what that means.

## Global facts of life

Christians believe that life is programmed for love. We are
created by Love for love. There is a commentary over the

start of the film *Love, Actually* in which the commentator says:

> Whenever I get gloomy about the state of the world, I think about the arrivals gate at Heathrow airport. General opinion is starting to make out that we live in a world of hatred and greed – but I don't see that. Seems to me that love is everywhere. Often it's not particularly dignified, or newsworthy – but it's always there. Fathers and sons, mothers and daughters, husbands and wives, boyfriends and girlfriends, old friends. If you look for it, I've got a sneaking feeling you'll find that love, actually, is all around.

Yes – and Christians try to encourage our culture to believe that love is indeed the irreducible minimum, and is based on the core reality at the heart of life. Nevertheless, it's from similar airports around the world that terrorists have taken off to commit the most appalling atrocities. The iconic picture of a plane set against a clear blue sky, just about to fly into one of the World Trade Center towers, still chills the soul.

We are constant recipients of the most heart-breaking news reports. Our astonishing communications technology gives us almost instant access to tragedy. It may be a tsunami in Indonesia, an earthquake in Haiti, a massacre in Mumbai, a suicide attack in Afghanistan, a hurricane in New Orleans or any number of other shocking events. It can leave a sensitive person with the feeling that life is utterly insecure, random and irrational. Best to hunker down, believe nothing and trust no one. Least of all God. I remember one woman in the church I served in Taunton coming to me after a particularly terrible earthquake and saying that she was leaving the church. She was very honest – she could no longer believe in a God who would allow this kind of thing to happen to innocent people.

In his book *In God We Doubt*, John Humphrys writes out of his own personal experience.

I was a young man, not much more than a boy, when I watched the miners of Aberfan digging for the bodies of their children after the coal tip crushed their school. A few years later when I should have been enjoying Christmas Day with my young family in New York, I was watching weeping mothers trying to free the bodies of their children from the ruins of houses wrecked by an earthquake in Nicaragua. In various African countries I have seen children, all hope gone from their blank and staring eyes, slowly starving to death. In divided countries all over the world I have seen the bodies of young men horribly mutilated by other young men for no other reason than that they belonged to the wrong tribe or religion. And over and over again I was asking myself the other Big Question . . . where was God?[6]

It's the exposure of innocence to the world's evil machinery that can be most disconcerting of all. The film *The Boy with the Striped Pyjamas* tells of the eight-year-old son of the commandant of a Nazi concentration camp who befriends an eight-year-old Jewish boy through the wire surrounding the camp. Bruno thinks the camp is a farm and can't understand why his friend is always hungry and wears striped pyjamas. When the father of the Jewish boy disappears, Bruno burrows under the wire to join his young friend to help him find his father, only to find himself caught in a hut where everyone is being taken off to the gas chamber. Bruno's father is left with the appalling truth that the killing machine he was running to dispose of Jews has destroyed his own son too.

I can still remember a picture of one small child, alone and crying in a sea of famine, that encapsulated for me the unmitigated horror of one international disaster. The child was sitting in the middle of the road, crying his eyes out, with people walking past, no one paying him any attention at all. To this day I would love to know what happened to that little innocent. The betrayal of innocence is enough to make any sensitive person despair. And with such despair might go the disappearance of any sense of a loving God. We can be worn down by tragedy until the world appears to be a poor, blighted rock spinning in a cold, dark universe. The global facts of life can finally defeat us. Our trust in God crumbles away.

And yet the human spirit often seems to rise still higher than these terrible situations and tragic events. I am immeasurably moved by the story of Yosl Rakover, one of the last survivors of the Warsaw ghetto. (So many extraordinary stories have come out of the Holocaust.) Rakover realized that he would inevitably be killed by the artillery fire and shells exploding around him in the ghetto. He had lost his wife and six children in the horrors of the ghetto; one of them, ten-year-old Rachel, had been driven by starvation to escape at night to search for bread in the city's rubbish bins. She was discovered and pursued, but in her weakness she collapsed and 'the Nazis drove holes through her skull'. In his final hours Rakover decided to call God to account and wrote a letter that was later found in a bottle in the ruins of the ghetto, among charred stone and human bones. This is some of what he wrote:

I have followed Him, even when He pushed me away. I have obeyed His commandments, even when He scourged me for it. I have loved Him, I have been in love with Him and remained so, even when He made me lower than the dust, tormented me to death, abandoned me to shame and mockery . . . Here then are my last words to You, my angry God: None of this will avail You in the least! You have done everything to make me lose my faith in You, to make me cease to believe in You. But I die exactly as I have lived, an unshakeable believer in You. Praised be forever the God of the dead, the God of vengeance, of truth and judgement, who will soon unveil His face to the world again and shake its foundations with His mighty voice.

'Sh'ma Yisroel! Hear, Israel! The Lord is our God, the Lord
is one. Into Your hands, O Lord, I commend my soul.'[7]

How can you respond to such extraordinary faith? It echoes
exactly the words of Job, 'Though he kill me, yet I will trust in
him' (Job 13.15). The atheist must despair of such apparently
irrational trust. It surely points to depths and reasons of the
heart of which the mind has little understanding. Yet to most
people the challenge of these tragedies is a compelling case
at least for doubt, and certainly for a reappraisal of the cuddly
versions of God's providential care for his people. And some
find their finger-tip hold on faith finally slips away.

## Communal facts of life

One further type of experience needs mentioning. People can
find their trust in God badly eroded by communal disappointment. A church community – large, vibrant, well led, and full
of faith – was hit by several personal tragedies that affected
everybody. First a little boy was taken seriously ill. The church
prayed and fasted; there were half-nights of prayer; there were
great statements of faith and prophecies that the little boy would
be healed. But still the boy got worse. The praying became more
intense as the stakes rose higher. There were vigils of prayer,
laying on of hands, more claiming of healing for him. The
little boy died. The church was thrown into bewilderment and
questioning, and the leaders tried to make the best of a bad
job with some fast theological footwork that barely patched
over the wound.

Not very long afterwards the assistant vicar's husband became seriously ill with cancer. They had young children and
he was well known and much loved in the church. Again the
faithful resources of the church were turned on this desperate
situation. All the stops were pulled out as the church prayed
again, but again, the priest's husband died. These situations test

the faith of the most confident Christian. At the very least they may loosen the conventional moorings, and an individual's ship of faith can find itself out in deeper waters, where either that faith proves itself in those much more demanding conditions or it's shipwrecked and lost.

## The consequences

The result of these tragic facts of life, whether personal, global or communal, is that many people are thrown into spiritual confusion. The God they thought they knew and trusted has suddenly gone quiet; the lines are down; there's no reassuring signal. And the reason is that human beings are a psycho-social unity. Mind, body, spirit and context all hang together. If the emotions are torn ragged by a relationship in crisis, then the spirit is damaged too. If the body is struggling to cope with an invasion of disease, then the prayer life suffers with it. If we're living under a heavy blanket of depression, it diminishes our capacity to receive any light from heaven.

Searching for intellectual answers is beyond us in such situations. It's not a time when we can cope with the idea of a God who, in the act of creation – as in every act of creativity from pottery to childbirth – has to limit himself in order to bring into being the thing created; a God who restricts his power in the interests of love. When you have a child you have *this particular* child, not some idealized Child. When you paint a picture you have *this* picture and not a thousand other ones that might be in your head. When God creates a universe it works according to *these* principles, not some other hypothetical ones. Creation involves giving up omnipotent possibilities and making something particular. Worthwhile existence requires genuine freedom not just for humans but also for the physical environment in which, and out of which, they have evolved. So the grinding of tectonic plates that results in earthquakes and tsunamis is as much a necessary part of Love's project as the freedom of a man to love a woman. But following that argument through makes the brain ache, and at the time of distress everything else is aching quite sufficiently without looking for any more bewilderment.

What Paul says of the whole body of Christ also applies to the individual Christian who follows him. 'If one member suffers, all suffer together with it' (1 Cor. 12.26). If one part of us hurts, so do the other parts. We may wish it could be otherwise and that the tragic facts of life would call out our most robust faith and our most vivid awareness of God, but the truth is that such heroics might often be quite short-lived or shallow. We usually have to suffer the weight of the problem before God can begin to infiltrate our new mental and emotional landscape. We usually have to be *sub-merged* before we can *re-merge* with him again.

After all, that was the route Jesus himself had to take all alone, one desperate weekend in Jerusalem.

# 4

## *The chattering culture*

In Nietzsche's *The Gay Science* the madman lights a lantern in the bright morning and runs to the market place to proclaim the death of God to scoffing bystanders. He realizes, however, that he has come too early and so he says: 'My time is not yet. This tremendous event is still on its way, still wandering; has not yet reached the ears of men.'[1] It seems, though, that this 'tremendous event' might be reaching us now. The word is on the street that God may not exist after all. Indeed it has become the default setting of the media and the chattering classes, and increasingly the implicit assumption of large sections of society.

The writer Minette Marrin pointed out in an article in the *Sunday Times*:

> It is a curious thing about religious people, but they seem to imagine that everybody, believer or not, thinks that Christianity is basically rather nice and good and provides, as the archbishop says, 'space' to think about humanity. They fail completely to understand that agnostics and atheists do not want religion – they find it intellectually incoherent and like Laplace, the French scientist, 'feel no need of that hypothesis'. They cannot forget the evil that has been done in the name of organised religion and may actually disapprove of it. They fear blind, irrational faith. The suggestion of bringing religion back into politics is genuinely quite shocking to them. For some non-believers it summons up the stench of theocracy and the burning of flesh.[2]

This context of functional or aggressive atheism can have a wearying and undermining effect on believers. In a lecture in 2009 Chief Rabbi Jonathan Sacks said:

> How can anyone still need religion if: to explain the universe we have science; to control the universe we have technology; to negotiate power we have politics; to achieve prosperity we have economics. If you're ill you go to a doctor, not a priest. If you feel guilty you go to a psychotherapist, not to confession. If you are depressed you take Prozac and not the book of Psalms. And if you seek salvation you go to our new cathedrals, namely shopping centres, where you can buy happiness at extremely competitive prices.[3]

No wonder the choice of holding a religious belief can seem both backward and eccentric.

## A grown-up world

Surely, many think, we live in a world that has grown out of religion. It had its uses when we thought there needed to be some meaning to life, but now we see the mindless universe for what it is. Richard Dawkins wrote in *Unweaving the Rainbow* that in the universe 'there is at bottom no design, no purpose, no evil, no good, nothing but pointless indifference'.[4] Now we've got that settled, we can get on with living courageously in the darkness.

The advertising guru Charles Saatchi offered his wisdom on the Ten Commandments. He said they are, 'An overrated lifestyle guide, unsustainable and largely ineffective, only succeeding in making people confused and guilty.' When questioned about which of the seven deadly sins he is guilty of he replied, 'All of them. And they are far from being sins. Rather, they are all very uplifting and create a balanced and engaged life.' When pushed on how to be more content and fulfilled he answered:

Are you careful to put other people first? Are you anxious about other people's happiness and wellbeing? Are you a caring listener and a reliable friend? If you have answered yes to any of the above, I believe we have pinpointed your first mistake . . . Only when you accept that much of the pleasure of being alive is to enjoy your own horribleness and the character flaws around you will you find harmony and each day will pass more sweetly.[5]

Perhaps this is what Nietzsche had in mind when he wrote, 'Was it not necessary to sacrifice God himself and then to worship stone, stupidity, gravity and fate.'[6]

A grown-up world can be quite condescending to God and to those who believe in God. When A. A. Gill was interviewed for the *Observer* by Lynn Barber, Gill wrote that she

did the Columbo thing of being gauche and cunningly hopeless. 'Sorry, I know I'm being stupid but can you tell me again: how bad a junkie were you?' I don't make a habit of talking about my days of wine and poppies. It's not that I mind people knowing, or that I'm ashamed of them, it's just that if there's one thing more boring than listening to a drunk, it's listening to a reformed drunk. In passing, really without thinking, I mentioned that I was a Christian.

Well that did it. Lynn almost inhaled her asparagus, her eyebrows shot off the top of her head. Nostrils bulging, she waved her arms as if for a passing lifeboat. 'A Christian,' she gasped, Lady Bracknell style, 'A Christian, as in believing in God, the God, that God?' Oh dear. Yes, that God. 'You're not, you can't possibly be.' Now remember she'd just found out that I'd been a drug dealer, spent adult years wetting beds, smoking cigarettes out of the gutter, sleeping in dog baskets, drinking Benylin and vodka through a straw for breakfast and seeing spiders the size of Vanessa Feltz's head, all of which had elicited no more than an encouraging ho-hum. This, after all, was only the tired, repetitive litany of contemporary celebrity revelation, but being a Christian and working in the media in the 21st century – being someone who's been to the Groucho, eats at the Ivy, is known to public relations VIP lists – how could you possibly be anything as embarrassingly naff and hick and unbelievable as a believer? Well, there it is. I'm outed, proud to be godly.[7]

Such an article is rare. Many more seem to make declaring one's lack of belief an essential disclaimer. Interestingly, however, what often accompanies this unbelief is a certain wistfulness. The writer Julian Barnes expresses this well in his book *Nothing to be Frightened of,* when he starts:

I don't believe in God, but I miss him . . . I miss the New Testament God rather than the Old Testament one. I miss the God that inspired Italian painting and French stained glass, German music and English chapter houses, and those tumble-down heaps of stone on Celtic headlands which once were symbolic beacons in the darkness and the storm.

Later he writes:

God is dead and without Him human beings can get up off their knees and assume their full height; and yet this height turns out to be quite dwarfish. Religion used to offer consolation for the travails of life, and reward at the end of it for the faithful. But above and beyond these treats, it gave human life a sense of context, and therefore seriousness . . . But was it true? No. Then why miss it? Because it was a supreme fiction, and it is normal to feel bereft on closing a great novel.[8]

Sadly, driven by our colossal technological success and believing our own inflated publicity, we have believed that God can be deposited in the archives of discarded anthropology. In a magazine article, Philip Pullman said of God: 'Poor old thing. He's got Alzheimer's, you know. He's suffering from billions of years of senile decay.'[9]

One theologian who saw this cultural shift coming was Dietrich Bonhoeffer. Later hanged by the Germans for taking part in the abortive attempt to assassinate Hitler in 1944, he wrote in his *Letters and Papers from Prison*:

> God lets himself be pushed out of the world and onto the cross. He is weak and powerless in the world, and that is precisely the way in which he is with us and helps us . . . The Bible directs man to God's powerlessness and suffering, for only the suffering God can help.[10]

This understanding of God requires a degree of theological sophistication that passes most people by. The common assumption is that if God is God at all, he must be strong and mighty, approximating (with a little room for metaphor) to the images of God in popular iconography and classic paintings. Not so, says wise theology; look deeper. God doesn't need to defend himself. God's chosen vulnerability is seen in the manger and on the cross. This is a God whose ways are not those of naked power but of inexhaustible love.

Christians will say that if we think we've outgrown this endless Source of love we could be heading for a deep, dark abyss. It's a risk that few cultures have entertained at any time throughout the colourful history of humankind, but it's one that is being advocated strongly in contemporary Western society.

## A scientific world

One major sub-set of this grown-up world is the scientific world-view that, for many, has dealt belief a death blow. Atheists such as Richard Dawkins, Peter Atkins, Christopher Hitchens and Daniel Dennett consider their un-belief to be self-evident. They rail against God with a kind of intellectual equivalent of road-rage. The Nobel laureate Steven Weinberg said: 'The world needs to wake up from the long nightmare of religious belief and anything we scientists can do to weaken the hold of religion should be done, and may in fact be our greatest contribution to civilisation.'[11] Peter Atkins believes the same: 'Science and religion cannot be reconciled, and humanity should begin to appreciate the power of its child and to beat off all attempts at compromise. Religion has failed, and its failures should stand exposed. Science . . . should be acknowledged king.'[12]

Sometimes the attack on God is so strident you simply have to stand and applaud the apopleptic strength of the invective. Richard Dawkins says of the Old Testament God that he 'is arguably the most unpleasant character of all fiction; jealous and proud of it; a petty, unjust, unforgiving control freak; a vindictive, blood-thirsty ethnic cleanser; a misogynistic, racist, infanticidal, gen-ocidal, filicidal, pestilential, megalomaniacal, sadomasochistic, capriciously malevolent bully.'[13] You have to hope, for Richard Dawkins' sake, that he's not going to meet that God when he dies!

However, the point for us to note is the effect this unremit-ting assault may have on the believer, particularly one who has not read the robust responses of scientists (such as John Lennox), philosophers (such as Keith Ward), theologians (such as Alister McGrath), social scientists (such as Kathleen Jones), literary critics (such as Terry Eagleton), and others too numerous to mention. Constant exposure to ridicule can make some dig in for rebellion and others lose confidence. The idea of God can become less vivid, praying can become less intimate, worship on Sunday morning can become less alluring. It's the gradual wearing away of a robust faith, like the erosion of a stone statue by exposure to acid rain.

Other thinkers are more tentative in their judgements. Julian Barnes again:

If everything still moves without a Prime Mover, why should it be less wonderful and less beautiful? Why should we be children needing the teacher to show us things, as if God were some superior version of a TV wildlife expert? The Antarctic penguin, for instance, is just as regal and comic, just as graceful and awkward, whether pre- or post-Darwin. Grow up, and let's examine together the allure of the double helix, the darkling glimmer of deep space, the infinite adjustments of plumage which demonstrate the laws of evolution, and the packed, elusive mechanism of the human brain. Why do we need some God to help us marvel at such things? We don't. Not really. And yet. If what is out there comes from nothing, if all is unrolling mechanically according to a programme laid down by nobody, and if our perceptions of it are mere micro-moments of biochemical activity, the mere snap and crackle of a few synapses, then what does this sense of wonder amount to? Should we not be a little more suspicious of it?[14]

The first order question remains: why is there anything rather than nothing? And where does the deep rationality of the universe come from, which enables rational beings to engage with it? As Professor Paul Davies writes:

> Atheists claim that the laws exist without reason and that the universe is ultimately absurd. As a scientist I find this hard to accept. There must be an unchanging rational ground in which the logical ordered nature of the universe is rooted.[15]

Believers will say that science is particularly well equipped to answer questions about 'how' things come to be as they are, while religion and philosophy specialize in answering questions about purpose, the 'why' questions. Science tends to work from the bottom up and religion from the top down, but the reality they describe is the same. After all, there are different types of knowledge with complementary languages. Scientific language is wonderful at opening up horizons of descriptive understanding, but ethical, aesthetic and personal knowledge require different languages. A poet will describe a rose differently from a botanist; a chemist will describe what happens in a kiss differently from a bride.

Contemporary Western science was born out of a Christian faith that pursued truth. The early scientists expected to find laws in nature because they believed in a lawgiver. In Kepler's famous words, science was about 'thinking God's thoughts after him'. Galileo, Pascal, Newton, Faraday, Mendel, Pasteur, Kelvin – all were theists, as are very many contemporary scientists. Many scientists and theologians would say that the religion and science disputes of the nineteenth century have transmuted into common intellectual enquiry about such things as the deeply ordered nature of the physical universe or the ethical use of our extraordinary technological capability. The problem, however, lies in the unfiltered deluge of non-theistic assumptions that still descend constantly on to Western minds. It leads many to loosen their hold on God.

## Consumer-driven world

There is another major cultural pressure on Western believers, and it's the religion of shopping. Westerners are obsessed with consumption and the need to own more and own bigger. Fashion, narcissism and novelty, together with a desire to construct our own reality, drive forward a vast High Street empire of consumption. I recognize it in my own attitude when under pressure: buying another book (or three) will restore my balance, 'make me feel human again'. At this point in writing I went to count how many pullovers I have in my wardrobe. The answer is 21, plus 7 sweatshirts for the summer. Why do I need 28 pullovers? Even if some are 15 years old and I can't bear to part with them, I can only wear one at a time.

With greater affluence has come the enthronement of choice in our culture. We have a 'must-fit-me-exactly' world-view. In his book *Globalisation: The Human Consequences*, Zygmunt Bauman argues that we have moved in Western culture from 'the satisfaction of need', through 'the promotion of desire', to 'satisfying our every wish'.[16] I must have a range of choices because it's my right as a consumer and so that I can create the 'me' I want to project to the world. Identity in the West today is based much more on style than on the traditional categories of class and religion.

The result is that Westerners live in a context where the harsher realities of life are kept at bay by a vast cushion of consumer goods. We are surrounded by 'stuff', and the more 'stuff' we have, like a man drinking salt water, the more we want. Other civilizations and former ages would have had to face the big questions of life and loss, of meaning and hope, with the basic resources to hand – family, community, their religious framework. Today we increasingly try to buy our way out of trouble or anxiety about our identity with new clothes, furniture, gadgets, holidays, and now the latest fad – 'experiences', purchased off the revolving display unit in W. H. Smith. The eternal verities of religion are superseded by the passing 'high' of commercial transaction. It can have a deadening effect on our spiritual life when we start coming to the High Street for inspiration rather than to church.

Every so often it seems as if the economic and financial system tries to right itself according to a wider framework of values. In other words, the system breaks down. It demonstrates that hubris and greed is not a long-term strategy for health, and gives society a chance to 'turn again' (repent) and construct a framework of longer-lasting values. One such correction happened in 2008, leading into the recession of 2009. Jonathan Sacks wrote about it at the end of that year:

Oscar Wilde was right when he defined a cynic as one who knows the price of everything and the value of nothing. The richer Britain became, the more cynical it grew. It put its faith in a financial house of cards. It looked at house prices and thought itself rich. It created the religion of shopping, whose 'original sin' was not having this year's must-have, and whose salvation lay in spending money you don't have, to buy things you don't need, for the sake of a happiness that doesn't last.[17]

The danger is that as a global community we may not be prepared to learn the lessons. The stuttering progress made at Kyoto, Bali and Copenhagen on reducing our consumption of fossil fuels for the sake of the planet suggests that nations are not yet prepared to ease back the throttle. What is true at the personal level appears to be echoed at the international level. The voice of God is being drowned out by the greed in our hearts and the seductive music in the shopping malls.

And underneath all that noise is the sad, silent fact that Christian believers also are sometimes losing touch with the sacred centre of their lives, finding that a relationship with a credit card is more instantly rewarding than a relationship with God. Bit by bit, God slips from the centre of the picture and is left apparently hanging on to the edge while we rush past muttering about how little time we have. The story is told of Rabbi Levi Yitzhak of Berditchev looking out over the town square and seeing people rushing about everywhere. He called out to one man, 'What are you rushing for?' and the man replied, 'To make a living.' The rabbi said, 'What makes you so sure that your livelihood is in front of you so that you have to rush to catch it up? What if it's behind you? Maybe you should stop and let it catch up with you.'

Perhaps there is wisdom there for our fast, instant, consumer-driven culture.

## The effect

We are thinking about how people lose the immediacy of their relationship with God and find their faith dropping down the list of their priorities. God 'whose glory fills the skies' can become the God we go to visit on Sunday mornings if we're not too tired from the week before. Tolstoy's picture of a passionate God, 'without whom one cannot live', can too easily become an anaemic concept of divine benevolence – shortly before that idea too slips out of the back door. The majestic picture of God as active, committed and present at every point can come under threat from the drip-effect of a chattering culture that believes it's grown up, science based, and consumer led, and has no need of God. And that can lead, for some, to the unravelling of the faith they have held and tried to live by.

Two stories may round out the picture. In our relativistic culture, almost anything goes. Committed belief is seen as somewhat quaint, or worse. So in Joanne Harris' book *Chocolat*, the main character, Vianne, is talking to her friend Guillaume:

'I don't think there is such a thing as a good or bad Christian,' I told him. 'Only good or bad people.' He nodded and took the little round pastry between finger and thumb. 'Maybe. In that case, the things I've believed in all my life – about sin and redemption and the mortification of the body – you'd say none of those things mean anything, wouldn't you?' I smiled at his seriousness. 'I'd say you've been talking to Armande,' I said gently. 'And I'd also say that you and she are entitled to your beliefs. As long as they make you happy.'

'Oh.' He watched me warily, as if I were about to sprout horns. 'And what – if it isn't an impertinent question – what do you believe?'

'Magic carpet rides, rune magic, Ali Baba and visions of the Holy Mother, astral travel and the future in the dregs of a glass of red wine. Buddha, Frodo's journey into Mordor. The transubstantiation of the sacrament. Dorothy and Toto. The Easter Bunny. Space aliens. The Thing in the closet. The Resurrection and the Life at the turn of a card. I've believed them all at one time or another. Or pretended to. Or pretended not to. And now? What do I believe right now?

'I believe that being happy is the only important thing,' I told him at last. Happiness. Simple as a glass of chocolate or tortuous as the heart. Bitter. Sweet. Alive.[18]

It's a perfect illustration of the tolerant, non-judgemental, chill-out ideology of our time. No need to get committed to a single set of beliefs. Why would you? Believe what you like and do what you like, as long as it doesn't hurt others. Surely that's enough.

The other story comes from Melvyn Bragg's book, *Remember Me*, in which Joseph, a believer, is with his French, non-believing wife, Natasha, in Notre Dame. Natasha is speaking:

'Yes. We know that God does not send down plagues. Plagues come from viruses. We know that God does not cause floods or famines. We know that if there is such a God,' she turned to him, her face set, 'I know that if there is such a God I want nothing to do with him and I will certainly not bow to him or worship a monster who creates a world like this one.' She paused and smiled. 'Poor Joseph. You don't like this.'

Joe was offended but he was also impressed. 'So what do you believe in?' 'Why do I have to believe?' 'If you don't believe in anything, what's the point?' 'I do not like this word. But if you force me to use it, I believe in you and me, Joseph. I believe that we should help François. I believe that some people I have known were cruel and hateful. I believe the world is full of wrong but some right too, but I don't need the pomp of Notre Dame for that. Notre Dame gets in the way. It is too complicated. It is a dicta-torship of belief. It takes us up too many unnecessary paths.'

'So the flying buttresses are just an accident?'

'A glorious accident, Joseph.'[19]

For Natasha and those like her there is no need for belief, and religious institutions are dictatorships. And that can undermine the vitality of faith for some believers who have lived confidently thus far within the embrace of the Christian faith. A chill wind blows in, bringing doubt from a far country. The faith that was the ground and granite of their being is being broken up.

## The role of doubt

Doubt is therefore the predominant belief in our culture. However, the opposite of doubt isn't faith; it's certitude, and we live in a culture dangerously obsessed with certitude. The writer Howard Jacobson pointed out in a university sermon the paradox that

> so many men of religious conviction are men [*sic*] of doubt, and so many doubters are men of utter certainty . . . The great failure of secularity as a guiding principle is that it does the opposite of what it says on the packet – it doesn't liberate or enlarge us, it confines us to certainty.[20]

It's those who have the truth captured, stuffed and mounted on the wall who are most scary, whether their certainty is about politics, the Second Coming, or assisted suicide. Premature certainty is corrosive of the humble pursuit of truth. Many issues need time for reflecting, pondering, discussing, leaving for a while, broadening out, deepening and so on. Rushing to judgement may be attractive, but it often leads to great error.

Doubt isn't the same as cynicism. Cynicism sees doubt as an end in itself, something in which to glory and to exploit. But honest doubt is a seeking, a desiring, a longing for understanding and wisdom. Ian Hislop, editor of *Private Eye*, once wrote:

> One of the first times I ever appeared on radio I got into a discussion and the presenter said, 'But you're not a Christian.' 'No,' I laughed. The cocks didn't crow but I felt

curiously disappointed with myself. At the time I was not sure whether I could be classified as a Christian or not. I didn't really believe but I didn't really not believe. I supposed I believed in belief. I feel much the same now. A life of doubt diversified by faith is roughly as far as I have got. I don't know which colour the chessboard is [white or black]. I don't know. I've sat in churches thinking this is all rubbish. And at other times I have felt that this is all there is. I don't know. I don't know.[21]

Here is honest doubt – searching, not disparaging; desiring, not ridiculing. There is a spectrum of doubt. At one end is the cynical, self-serving doubt that doesn't know, and therefore seeks to destroy. Further along the spectrum is the honest doubt of Ian Hislop, admitting the mystery, the not-knowing, and staying open to the question. But further along again is the doubt of the believer, the place where many of us are at some point of time in our pilgrimage. And here doubt can be a healthy ingredient of faithful living.

The doubt of the believer is like the roots of a tree searching down into the depths of the earth, going in entirely the opposite direction to that of the tree. But only because those roots are deep is the tree secure from the blasts of winter. Shallow roots would be ripped up. The deep roots of doubt, going apparently in the opposite direction to faith, are actually a guarantee against immaturity and the premature shipwreck of faith. To have entered the zone of dark doubt is to have had to face the demons, the negative arguments, the wondering 'if this was all folly', and to have found an accommodation, a way of staying in there.

The philosopher Unamuno wrote, 'Those who believe they believe in God but without passion in the heart, without anguish of mind, without uncertainty, without doubt and even at times without despair, believe only in the idea of God, not in God himself.'[22] And Dostoevsky, too, wrote, 'It is not as a child that I believe and confess Jesus Christ. My *hosanna* is born of a furnace of doubt.'[23] Of course there is no particular virtue in seeking out and nurturing doubt but it need not be something to fear. As Matthew says when the disciples are gathered on a mountain in Galilee and about to bid Jesus farewell, 'When they saw him, they worshipped him; but some doubted.' In a sermon in Cambridge, Lord Blair, former Metropolitan Commissioner, cleverly applied the mind of a detective to the foundations of the Christian story, and he spoke of doubt as 'a necessary accompaniment of Christian faith, the mortar of intelligence in the wall of belief'.[24] As such, doubt is what keeps believers grounded and, at its lowest, prevents silliness.

I once accompanied a lovely couple in their latter days. He was a priest, she a wonderfully resourceful founder of homeless charities. When she died, the priest wrote:

> I continue to read the office and tell God every Sunday that I am a believer for the next week. I suspect he's more amused than impressed and, by now, getting bored. But I still have this feeling that I must keep faith with [Helen] whose last words were, 'I don't think there's a god there. He hasn't helped me.' But lately I've had one or two intimations, as Wordsworth would say, that I interpret as indicating that things may be sorted out. It could be imagination of course, but for the moment I go along with them.

Different positions, but coming out of a common pool of uncertainty. The mood of our culture is distinctly sceptical and many faithful believers have been undermined by a continual diet of secularist opinions. They have been told that we live in a grown-up world without need for God, that we live in a scientific world where belief in God is no longer possible, and that we live in a consumerist world where God doesn't need to be on the shelves. It adds up to a depressing verdict on faith for many believers and the reality of God's felt presence in their lives gradually ebbs away.

So what now?

# 5

## *Surviving the darkness*

————•◦•————

I'm writing this on Christmas Eve. Snow is lying thickly outside and all the anticipation of seasonal celebration is in the air. Our family is arriving soon in the shape of our grown-up children, now with their own small wriggly offspring. The larder is full and the television waits expectantly, not having been used very much through the autumn. The atmosphere is not of darkness but of light. Sparkling Christmas tree lights reflect the air of expectancy that runs through the whole house.

And yet it's at such times that those who have lost their first love of God can feel most in darkness. The church family is all a-quiver with the joy of Christmas, while they are out in the cold wondering 'Where did all the love go?' Times of celebration are most clearly the times of exclusion, and that applies, of course, just as much to those who are bereaved, seriously ill or in troubled relationships – they too suffer more acutely at a time of general celebration.

To a lesser degree, every Sunday can seem like that to someone who is in the twilight of their faith. Sunday mornings used to seem so charged with energy and anticipation. The Christian family was gathering from all around the place, people who had lived their discipleship dispersed throughout the community during the week and were now coming together to celebrate all that God had done. Yet for the spiritually dispossessed it's now a time of nostalgia, either going along and smiling through a mask, or being absent and wondering how to fill these unusual hours.

The abiding question lies unanswered: OK, God has gone absent; now what?

## *Olives and sour wine*

One of the resources to pull out of the rucksack when we are in this darkness is the experience of Jesus in his last 24 hours. How seriously do we take the absences that Jesus went through? His hours among the olive trees of Gethsemane were not play-acting. If you sweat with what seems like drops of blood you're in a bad place (Luke 22.44). Jesus wasn't losing touch with his Father but he was in a different kind of spiritual freefall. Every hope he had entertained, that his people would recognize God's moment when it came, was lurching wildly away from him. The people were not going to respond to the message of the kingdom; they were going to carry on as usual and he alone would be left standing – or rather hanging. What was he to do? This was a return to the earliest days of being tempted to find easier methods and short cuts, temptations he thought he'd dealt with on a desert retreat three years ago. But nothing had changed; human nature was as dull and short-sighted as ever. Everyone else had stepped back; he alone was left in line and the result was becoming obvious.

It got even worse a few hours later. Jesus was hammered mercilessly on to a cross and as he hung there between heaven and earth it seemed to Jesus that heaven itself had closed its doors, that there was no one listening. His Father had left him to it; there was no comfort from the Source of Life from whom he had drawn his energy and inspiration throughout his life. It seemed that his life was now just draining away. There was nowhere else to go but death.

## *And yet . . .*

And yet Jesus still addressed his Father, still spoke to him as one who was present, even in his absence. He spoke into the darkness. He refused to admit he'd got it all wrong. He just wanted to know why his Father had gone silent. He wanted to protest with every ounce of strength he had left, to cry to heaven 'Why? Why?' But still he spoke.

Will we still speak into the darkness?

## *Being honest*

This is the first thing to promise ourselves – to be honest about what is happening. There is a peculiar kind of Christian conspiracy to pretend to ourselves that God is in heaven and all is right with the world, even if we have had no evidence of that for the last six months. But we'll get nowhere until we've come to admit that there's a problem. It was only when I started to tell my spiritual director that I was frustrated with God's silence that we could begin to look at the dynamics of my relationship with God. What was I expecting God to do? Was that reasonable? Was I actually being honest with God myself and was I taking the dark material to him as well? Honesty is the bass line of any relationship of quality.

A pupil at a school I was connected with was very angry about his parents splitting up. He heard a sermon about Jacob arguing and fighting with God through the night, so he went back to his room and burst out, 'God, I hate you.' 'Excellent,' said his chaplain later. Why? Because he was being honest. The psalms are full of the passionate cries of honest people venting their feelings. God can handle that. It's the start of a refreshed relationship, free of the temptations of piety and good manners. If God has disappointed us by letting life go wrong or by wandering off, it's liberating to let him know.

## *'Don't panic'*

The famous catchphrase from *The Hitchhiker's Guide to the Galaxy* applies directly to the person who has lost contact with the living God. There's lots to be done before panicking. Problems usually come to us as a lump; the first task is to take the lump apart and see what it's made up of. In analysing the problem we're having with our spiritual life it helps to see how many elements are involved – maybe tiredness, or boredom, or the church, or problems in another area of life altogether. Rather than think that this spiritual journey was all folly it's valuable to break the dark lump down into its constituent parts and consider what could be done about its different elements.

As a matter of experience, panic isn't the most common response anyway. Loss of faith is more often the 'melancholy, long, withdrawing roar' of Matthew Arnold's Sea of Faith. People usually drift out of religious practice rather than go around consumed by existential angst, drawing others into a communal pit of misery. Indeed one of the problems in some communities is that people aren't noticed as they follow the tide out to sea. That can be a further disillusioning experience: 'They didn't even notice!' But, if they do notice, we might have to duck. We might be subject to the assault troops of pastors, apologists and Job's Comforters who all move in with The Answer, and leave you wondering who's panicking now.

There's no need, either way. Stay cool. There's a process going on here, not a single event.

## *Praying into emptiness*

This is where we might draw on the experience of Jesus on the cross. He lost God but he prayed. He threw his protest into the empty skies, refusing to believe that the One who had deserted him was not there for him in some way. So it is with us. At the same time as giving up other religious practices like churchgoing, we may still feel we want to keep referring events to God, or referring God's absence to God! It's part of that natural instinct to pray which exists in a huge majority of the population of every land. We seem to be hard-wired for prayer along a whole range of expressions, from the set forms of liturgical prayer to the most tentative practice of 'thinking in the direction of

God'. Our experiences of gratitude, wonder, sorrow and need all seem to draw out of us an instinctive response of prayer, which is then 'stretched out' by some of us as a more intentional discipline and privilege.

So prayer is harder to stop than belief – and my encouragement would be not to try. Praying into the darkness may seem futile at one level, but it keeps open the possibility that normal service will be resumed. Or rather, that a 'new normal' service may be resumed, because it is unlikely that anything will be the same after a significant crisis of faith. Prayer is such a multi-layered gift it's hard to believe there isn't some expression of it that won't be possible for everyone with some inkling of the spiritual.

For some of us, sitting in silence is going to be the most that we are able to do. Archbishop Rowan Williams was in conversation with the writer Diana Athill on BBC Radio 4 after Christmas in 2010 and they had been talking about 'what is there', which Diana Athill found sufficient in itself and the Archbishop believed led on to further discovery. He said:

> When you open up in silence to what is there, there is something there that is not yourself which you struggle to find images and words for, which comes into focus for me as a Christian dramatically and decisively in one set of stories. But behind that is an infinite hinterland – you open up, you're silent, you seek to absorb what is there. And that's the root of serious religious practice. It's looking down and down and down to something that doesn't have a bottom, a final point of explanation, but seeing that that very infinity somehow opens out on to what I call God, who is the context, the environment in which everything makes sense, the bottomless Resource of action, intelligence and love.

This silent abstraction may be the only place of refuge for the believer who has lost touch with God, and it might open up into 'a context, an environment' in which something begins to make sense. But if we don't stay there we'll never know. My strong suggestion is that we don't turn away too soon. Jesus prayed into emptiness and the habits of a lifetime did not play him false. Three days later his persistence was gloriously vindicated.

## *Friends and good companions*

The most important resource we have when spiritual things have gone dark is other people. The tragedy is that the people who are most important to us, and potentially most helpful, are often precisely the people we don't feel we can turn to. We're embarrassed, perhaps a little ashamed. This is tender ground, perhaps even a swamp into which good friendships might sink and be lost. Best to keep it to myself, I think; maybe my actions will give the game away and I won't have to talk about it openly.

At some level, however, most of us long to offload the pain and confusion. If we scan the full range of our friends and family perhaps we will be able to identify the one person who we know, at some deep instinctive level, will be able to hold our confusion. It might be quite a surprise to realize who that person is. It often works at a level of recognition beyond the rational mind. That person will be safe; he or she won't have the Answer – there are no silver bullets. But that person will be a listener who doesn't judge, a companion who doesn't force the pace, a wise friend who absorbs whatever you give him or her. Just ask.

Some people have spiritual directors or soul friends who have established themselves as people who have those qualities and also that crucial gift of impartiality, even objectivity. This relationship isn't one in which to play games. As I indicated above, it was when I could come clean about God's silence, both with my spiritual director and with a monk who was accompanying me on a silent retreat, that I began to loosen the debris that had set hard over the entrance to my spiritual 'mine-shaft'. Then light could begin to seep in again, and the fresh air of the Spirit.

Who would you talk to?

## *Remembering*

There probably is a place for remembering the good times, even if the memory is bitter-sweet. It reminds us that a different experience from the current darkness is at least possible. The danger is that we find ourselves in difficulty and proceed to throw off the past and reinterpret it as a long misjudgement, an immature mistake. That's what Andrew Motion did as described in Chapter 3. After the serious injury to his mother he found he no longer believed in God and after a week he wondered what all his previous religious devotion had been about.

This type of conversion *out of* faith is of course just as possible as a direct conversion *into* faith. But both moves need to be checked out, and memory is an important factor in this. Is every good experience of faith suddenly to be wiped out as meaningless? Was it all a glorious fantasy? Are all my Christian friends simpletons? As the immediate experience of God faded for me I remembered the times in worship that had moved me deeply, the times I had stood on mountain tops and praised the Creator, the reaching out of my whole being for God which came as an epiphany as well as a profound longing. These were welcome correctives to the anxiety that God could never again stir my soul to passion.

The psalmist remembered 'how I went with the throng, and led them in procession to the house of God, with glad shouts and songs of thanksgiving, a multitude keeping festival'. And so he went on, 'Why are you cast down, O my soul, and why are you disquieted within me? Hope in God; for I shall again praise him, my help and my God' (Ps. 42.4, 5).

Memory can keep us anchored. It can restrain us from precipitate action, and remind us that there were good times of rich spiritual experience, and unless we wish to completely re-write the past, there was authenticity in those experiences. Love may come again.

## *Hoping*

As the verse from Psalm 42 said, it's possible to hope in God because of what we have known of God's ways in the past. Two of the most characteristic words in both Old and New Testaments are the words 'but' and 'nevertheless'. 'When my soul was embittered, when I was pricked in heart, I was stupid and ignorant; I was like a brute beast towards you. *Nevertheless* I am continually with you; you hold my right hand . . .' (Ps. 73.21–23). 'You have heard that it was said . . . *But* I say to you . . .' (Matt. 5.21–22). Those great words are statements of promise. The world may seem to be like *this*, but actually it's like *that*. Until now things have been going *this way*, but now, because of Jesus, they're going *that way*. The challenge is – believe the deeper story.

At the same time, hope is not blind. Miracles take time, so hope is a real piece of work, not just a positive state of mind. And it doesn't always result in a shining success story either. Vaclav Havel, the former President of the Czech Republic, once said, 'Hope is not the conviction that something will turn out well, but the certainty that something makes sense, regardless of how it turns out.'[1] When we have lost our living touch with God what we need isn't just a resumption of that old warm glow; it's the conviction that faith is a rational, wise choice and not merely whistling in the dark.

As a young priest in the early 1980s, I remember becoming very anxious about the possibility of a nuclear holocaust. International relations were in a bad way. There was much sabre rattling, but these sabres could cause a nuclear war and I wondered how I would look after my young family if someone made an idiotic move and the whole world order went into meltdown. I think I realized for the first time fully that God gives no guarantees against human stupidity. The radical nature of the freedom he gives has to include the freedom of accidents and idiocy, otherwise it's not freedom at all but just a lighter touch on the reins. And freedom is another name for love. Love releases and perfect love releases perfectly and fully. So my understanding of God's love became more nuanced. I had to see God's love as more extreme and dangerous than I'd believed. Existence is an adventure, and in an adventure there has to be the risk of both success and failure, or the adventure is just a charade. So if God might allow us to blow the world into a nuclear winter what did I have left? The answer was – hope. Not superficial optimism but rock-solid hope. The sort of hope that Paul talks about in Romans 8 where he states categorically that nothing can separate us from the love of God, 'neither death, nor life, nor angels, nor rulers, nor things present, nor things to come, nor powers, nor height, nor depth, nor anything else in all creation' (Rom. 8.38–39). Nothing.

And that sort of hope liberates people from the paralysing fear that stops them being able to tackle the actual spiritual problems they face. Hope is a core element of faith and it's one of the last things that should be lost when the windows of faith go dark.

## No guarantees

I realize that the strategies I have suggested above are merely good theory until placed on the anvil of our own loss of God. They may be empty words because it's the very nature of the problem that other people's experience isn't ours, and rational answers are simply like snowballs thrown into the fire. Nevertheless, if they give a hint of a hint of an approach, that would be fine for now.

But there's another field entirely to explore, and that's the possibility of reconstructing the edifice of faith using different materials. It's to this task that the second half of this book now turns. As football managers always say, it's a game of two halves and if the first half has gone against us, the second half is when we might look for a new shape to the team – and maybe a goal or two.

*Part 2*

# NEW BEGINNINGS

# 6

## *Re-imagining faith*

———•·•·•———

The time has come to begin some reconstructive surgery. It's all very well diagnosing the problem, but where do we now look to restore the fragile substance of the soul? One thing is certain: when the sun rises, it rises slowly. There'll be no quick fix to refill our spiritual sails. Like any strong natural process, healing the soul takes time.

Of course there are exceptions. We never quite know when God will turn up again, or awake us out of a long sleep. Sara Miles was a war journalist. She had been raised as an atheist and had never said the Lord's Prayer in her life. Then one winter morning she found herself walking into a church. 'It was all pretty peaceful,' she wrote, and then something happened that completely changed her life.

> We gathered around that table. And there was more singing and standing, and someone was putting a piece of fresh, crumbly bread in my hands, saying 'the body of Christ,' and handing me the goblet of sweet wine, saying 'the blood of Christ,' and then something outrageous and terrifying happened. Jesus happened to me. I still can't explain my first communion. It made no sense. I was in tears and physically unbalanced: it felt as if I had just stepped off a curb or been knocked over, painlessly, from behind. The disconnect between what I thought was happening (I was eating a piece of bread); what I heard someone else say was happening (the piece of bread was the 'body' of 'Christ,' a patently untrue or at best metaphorical statement); and what I

*knew* was happening (God, named 'Christ' or 'Jesus,' was real, and in my mouth) utterly short-circuited my ability to do anything but cry.[1]

It was the start of a complete personal makeover, and also led within a few years to her starting nearly a dozen food pantries in the poorest parts of the city. This, however, is the exception. For most of us the dawn comes slowly and it's only in stages that we notice the warmth creeping back into our chilled soul. The point I want to make in the second half of this book, however, is that although we can't make the sun rise any faster than it will, there are nevertheless things we can do to put ourselves in the way of its hopeful rays. The first one is a mind shift that re-imagines faith in several fundamental ways.

## Faith not as regulation but as relationship

As I think back to the faith I lived with through my childhood and teens, it seems to me that it was a religion of rules and regulations designed to save me from the worst excesses of myself. Not that I was on the verge of becoming a notorious drug dealer or a rampant danger to women, but I was held in a framework of moderate restraint, where the final sanction was a rather vague idea of God and an even vaguer concept of divine penalties. The great liberation which I discovered at university was a faith that was intellectually credible and emotionally satisfying, but which above all was based not on rule and regulation but on relationship and, indeed, love.

The problem I had was with religion as a human construct which had obscured faith as a transformative gift. Bishop John Saxbee defines religion as follows:

> Religion is the formalising of faith for a mixture of mo-
> tives and by means of, *inter alia*, doctrines and disciplines;
> credal statements and codes of behaviour; corporate mem-
> bership and rites of initiation; cultic practices and personnel;

legally constituted structures of organisation and authority; sacred scriptures, sites and symbols etc.[2]

None of this is bad in itself. Religion is necessary as a vehicle to pass on the divine treasure from one generation to another. It prevents chaos, and holds mavericks to account. It sponsors order instead of anarchy, providing frameworks that give people security in which they can grow and flourish. However, religion can be – especially for teenagers – a snare and a confusion.

The breakthrough comes when we let the butterfly of faith emerge from the chrysalis of religion, and see that faith is about relationship, encounter and presence before it's about concepts, arguments and structures. At root, faith is about union with the divine, the true goal of our stifled spirituality. God is the one we have been blindly seeking all along, confining him to a system of reasonable beliefs, checks and balances, when all the time God was wanting us to leap into a trusting relationship.

Indeed, the image of leaping is a powerful description of existential commitment. Picture the acrobat poised above the hushed tent, balanced, body tensed, ready for that leap into nothingness, trusting only in the outstretched hands of the catcher. There is nothing the acrobat can do but leap; everything depends on the catcher being there and being reliable. The Divine Catcher is utterly to be trusted, but how do you know that, when you stand 60 feet above the circus floor praying that what you are doing isn't completely absurd? The idea of the 'leap of faith' is sometimes ridiculed as an irrational choice to believe in what cannot be proved, but that isn't what the philosopher Kiekegaard thought it was at all. He maintained that religion could only be a penultimate giver of meaning, and that in order to get over the abyss of apparent meaninglessness one needs to take the leap of faith into the embrace of the everlasting arms. It means staking one's life on something which may be mistaken but which offers a life that is much more thrilling and redemptive than staying with the alternative world-view of a life without meaning or purpose.

By that leap we leave the old world of spiritual accountancy where the teenager (me) is caught up in guilt and debt, trying to keep the commandments, and we enter a new world of joyful union where the young man (me again) finds a shimmering depth in ordinary things. 'If anyone is in Christ, there is a new creation: everything old has passed away; see, everything has become new!' (2 Cor. 5.17). The key to this transformation is understanding faith as a relationship of intimacy with God in Christ – the usual word is 'union'. Religion then becomes less an arena of argument over ideas and doctrines and rather a crucible of relationships and divine presence. And that changes everything.

The Franciscan writer Richard Rohr gives a lovely image of this. He writes:

> I often notice young mothers in stores and supermarkets, and they are invariably some of the happiest people I meet. They often make eye contact and smile at you, and graciously apologise for being in your way. Why? Their constituting other [their point of reference] is absolutely clear and constant: their baby. Inside of that they know who they are, and they know exactly what their day's purpose is.[3]

He then notes that to Jewish believers there was always one face to which they would turn constantly for validation and definition – the face of God. 'Healthy religion creates very healthy people.' We are made healthy by being held in the gaze of God, just as we try to hold God in our own gaze.

Without that Significant Other, Rohr says, we have to be our own centre, or rather, 'our centre will change literally every few hours or even every few minutes, with every new celebrity, reputation, image, name, TV show, magazine article, billboard or love interest'. There may be an element of hyperbole here but Rohr is surely right that we need to be held in the loving gaze of the One who is our continual reference point in order to remain eternally steady. And our life task is to learn, bit by bit, to return the gaze of the One who loves us. Faith like this is a far cry from religion as a heavy package of rules and regulations. Can we trust that relational understanding of faith and turn away from religion as a restrictive system and towards God as our defining Other? As always, it's the direction of our gaze that matters.

## Faith not as arrival but as quest

When I was ordained part of me thought I'd arrived. All that study and preparation, all that prayer and anticipation, and now I had that strange white band around my neck. But I was 'only' a curate. So when I became a vicar, part of me thought I'd arrived. It's why I'd abandoned law after my first degree, after all, and it was what I'd been ordained for. I had a wonderful time as a vicar; everything we tried seemed to come off. But what would I then do with all that exciting experience? So I went to teach in a theological college and part of me thought I'd arrived. It was a time of great intellectual stimulus, but after a while I realized it was only engaging part of me and I wanted to be back out on the front line again.

So I went to be an archdeacon and part of me thought I'd arrived. After all, my title was on our medieval garden gate into the cloisters: 'Archdeacon of Canterbury'. I hoped people would notice. But then I realized I probably wouldn't be happy being an archdeacon for 17 years, so I was honoured when a bishop wrote and asked me to be his suffragan in the episcopal task – and part of me thought I'd arrived . . . Do you get the picture? We never 'arrive'. Christian faith is a journey, not an arrival. It's a quest, not a boxed set ('Everything You Need to Know about Being a Christian').

Christian living is being serious about the journey more than the ending. Of course the end matters because the goal is the vision and eternal presence of God. And of course it matters that we can have confidence – assurance – in God's saving love. But there is great danger in focusing exclusively on certainty about our Christian 'answers', about what is definitely right and definitely wrong, about who is 'in' and who 'out' in terms of eternal destiny. Certitude is seductive but ultimately danger- ous. Many books have been written by people who have escaped from fundamentalism, damaged and relieved. They had rightly valued the sense of assurance in emotional terms, but in intellec- tual terms certainty had led to much confusion and disillusion. In a bewildered age with postmodern commentators telling us that all truth claims are bids for power and there are no fram- ing stories (meta-narratives) that you can trust, it's easy to see the appeal of pre-modern certainties which seem to recapture the moral, spiritual and philosophical high ground.

John Saxbee has a helpful image.

In a large department store, you can choose whether to use the stairs or take the lift when making your way from floor to floor. Climbing the stairs will demand effort, and it will involve you being exposed to both the temptations and the delights of each successive department. Taking the lift is easier; as you occupy your secure little room you move through the various floors safe from involvement with any department with which you do not care to do business. The user of the lift, like many religious conserva- tives, inhabits a secure and unchanging environment, while on the stairs we see the theological liberals struggling to come to terms with each new department and having to decide how to spend what he or she has available and how to choose wisely from what is on offer. [As we move on in the twenty-first century] more and more people are being encouraged to take the safe and secure 'lift' of Christian conservatism – with the operators not so much telling the lift occupant what is available floor by floor, as telling the floor staff what is available in the lift![4]

The result of course is that while we travel up and down in our own little lifts, arguing about who should be let in, the rest of society is convinced the lift is out of order and gets on with the ordinary (but ultimately barren) activities of getting and spending. Our place is out on the shop floor! It seems to me that when we are looking for a way back, or a way in, to an intelligent and satisfying faith for today, what we need is a balance of confidence and humility, clarity and mystery, knowing and not knowing, outer truth and inner truth – committed, passionate balance.

It's interesting that in the Gospels Jesus doesn't seem to be interested in people's belief system. What matters to him is their relationship with the poor, with each other and with him. That does not mean that orthodoxy ('right thinking') doesn't matter; what it does mean is that we can't presume that we have all the answers about a God who is magnificently beyond human imagining. If our faith isn't humble we can end up being smug or even quite silly in what we believe and say. My experience is that those who are closest to God are always humble and those who are somewhat distant are usually quite sure of themselves. This humility reflects the humility of God, seen in the courtesy of Christ. It's often observed that the famous painting of Holman Hunt, *The Light of the World*, hanging in the chapel of Keble College in Oxford, shows Jesus knocking at a door without an outside handle. Jesus stands at the door knocking but only the person inside can open the door. God does not overwhelm us.

To take this point one stage further, the need for a certain diffidence in making assertions about Christianity means that when we speak about God our best language is likely to be in the form of metaphors and pointers. Words that assume too much clarity will end up dividing and confusing people or, as I suggested, sounding rather silly. The language of mystery and metaphor is more helpful. It allows for some opacity, some humility in the face of the God whose divine Word we see creating a universe and whose life extends beyond human comprehension.

Christian faith is therefore best seen as a quest for deep wisdom. To make it into a package of certainties is to demean the Creator and open ourselves to misunderstanding or irrelevance. If we have struggled with God, or lost sight and sound of God, perhaps it's worth stepping back from too much certainty and sense of 'arrival' and allowing faith to be a quest (and indeed a question). The honesty of the humbler path means that we can spend a lifetime on a journey of joyful exploration of a God who will always leave us speechless. The journey may well take us into the mystical way of silent encounter, when words fall away and Presence speaks straight to the heart. Or the journey may take us back to the person of Jesus, the person in whom the divine lightning finally struck the earth (of whom more later in Chapter 11). Either way, we can step back to a less assertive position and turn our longing gaze to a gentler God.

## *Faith not as success but as direction*

In Chapter 1 we encountered a number of ways in which the spiritual well runs dry. One of them was simple weariness after being on the Christian journey for a long time and running into the sand. This loss of passion can lead not only to spiritual lethargy but also to guilt and play-acting. We keep up appearances because it's too embarrassing to say that the substance has gone out of it, but in reality we've lost the burning faith of our younger days.

The way to tackle this vulnerability may lie first of all in understanding something of what's actually going on. This mid-life renegotiation (which may occur early or late – 'mid-life' is a season, not a date) is the time when we are starting to try and integrate our outer journey and our inner one. The 'ascent' of the early years is tipping over into the 'descent' of the later years. The time of ambition, of achieving, of making a mark, is being balanced by the time of facing limitations, interpreting the past, facing mortality, evaluating our worth. This is natural, important and not a reason to panic. Sadly, some of us regress at this point and do something erratic (the subject of many novels) and apparently 'completely out of character'. What's happening is that our 'character', built up through thousands of influences and tens of thousands of decisions, is now under serious review.

With such an understanding of what's going on, a Christian may then be tempted to think of returning to safe spiritual practices where prayer has been experienced as real in the past. It's probably true, however, that there is actually no way back, only a looking back in order to find a new way forward into uncharted spiritual territory, recognizing that God has moved on and is calling us to follow. This may be a time when we start looking to the quieter ways of faith, to the practice of stillness and silence, to the power of sacrament and symbol, to the fertility of mystery and paradox. It will almost certainly help to identify a mature spiritual friend as someone with whom to talk this process through. It may even help to break out of the limitations of over-familiar places and travel to a new physical space, thus making a deliberate move out of the spiritual torpor in which we have become encased. 'Place' is important. When I worked at Canterbury cathedral I once came across a man sitting ruminatively in the cloisters. I greeted him tentatively and he said immediately, 'A few years ago this place saved my life.' He repeated it: 'I came here when I was in trouble and this place saved my life.' I didn't intrude further; it was sufficient that this ancient house of prayer had done its job. Place matters.

Lasting faith doesn't depend on success; it depends on having a consistent direction which we try to follow even when energy levels are low and enthusiasm has hibernated. Success is a preoccupation of the first half of life and the second half is about heading patiently in the right direction – 'going home'.

The spiritual practices that feed us now might be very different from what we did at an earlier age, but they are none the worse for that. Continuing to wind ourselves up to achieve youthful spiritual ardour is a recipe for failure and increasing desperation. Let God take us forward with the manna we need for today; yesterday's manna has gone off.

## Faith not as locating God at a distance, but as recognizing God in the midst

In Chapter 1 we looked at the problem of people understanding God as so transcendent that he is beyond human knowing, which eventually can lead to us just getting on with life as if God were not there. God is left to the furthest reaches of his cosmic playground while we get on with running our lives as best we can. Omnipotence is thereby irrelevant.

The problem is that this emphasis on the transcendence of God is at the expense of another major biblical theme, that of God's intimacy and friendship. Moses talked with God, 'as one speaks to a friend' (Exod. 33.11). God is often depicted as intensely committed to his people, to the point of possessiveness. 'Do not fear, for I have redeemed you; I have called you by name, you are mine . . . you are precious in my sight, and honoured, and I love you' (Isa. 43.1, 4). Or simply: 'When Israel was a child, I loved him'. (Hos. 11.1). At its best Christian theology has always tried to hold together these themes of God's immense greatness and his intense intimacy.

To those, therefore, who are tempted to displace God to the outer regions of human imagination, it's necessary to offer the balancing truth that God is also closer to us than our own breath. God is not far away but right here. We live in him and he lives in us. The spiritual writer Martin Laird puts it beautifully: 'God does not know how to be absent. The fact that most of us experience throughout most of our lives a sense of absence or distance from God is the great illusion that we are caught up in.'[5] If God doesn't know how to be absent there's no need to chase him as if trying to capture an exotic animal. It's better to stay put because God never leaves home. If anyone is absent it's us – and with a culture of constant speed and trivial entertainment, that's not hard to imagine.

A variant on this problem of locating God unhelpfully is the second theological issue we encountered in Chapter 1, that of our desire for sensory experience of God. Many people long for something more tangible so that we can say that we have touched the edge of God's mystery and been burned by fire. We long for God to overwhelm us with his blistering reality, as the philosopher Pascal obviously once experienced. When he died his friends found sewn into his jacket a piece of paper describing something he wanted always to keep close to him. It said, 'Between nine o'clock and midnight. Fire! Not the God of the philosophers but the God of Abraham, the God of Isaac, the God of Jacob. Joy, joy, joy!' Isn't that what we all want? (Fortunately, we've still got Matins in the Church of England!)

However, the search for this kind of experience can become increasingly desperate, and it can become a kind of manipulation of God, trying to make God appear on demand to fit in with my spiritual needs. But still (I convince myself), isn't it reasonable to expect a bit of high-octane spiritual experience when we call on God? Why would God want to refuse it? Like C. S. Lewis we feel that we're doing all the pulling on the rope at our end – all we want is a bit of a twitch from the other end. Surely it isn't much to ask.

It is, however, a skewed theology that expects God to be found only in spectacular experiences and unusual events. It means we're happy when people get healed and when we get a chill up our spine during worship, but when nothing of note happens, then we pine for God to reveal himself.

The answer, I believe, is to resist the desire to manipulate God into making regular live appearances on our own stage, and instead to *recognize* the presence of God in the warp and weft of everyday life. God is a God of every last molecule of creation and so, by definition, God will be encountered much more often in the ordinary than in the spectacular, simply because there's so much more of it! Can we train ourselves to observe the depth of ordinary things? In Genesis 28 Jacob has a weird dream of a ladder set up between earth and heaven with angels floating up and down it, but in the morning he wakes from his sleep and says, 'Surely the Lord is in this place – and I did not know it!' He recognized the presence of God that he had previously not been able to see.

God inhabits every square centimetre of his creation. Scratch the surface of anything and God is to be found. But we have to train ourselves to notice, and that requires patient practice. Annie Dillard in one of her books writes that, when observing nature,

> It's all a matter of keeping my eyes open. Beauty and grace are performing there daily whether or not we'll sense them. The least we can do is try to be there . . . so that creation need not play to an empty house.[6]

Ian Markham takes this a stage further. He maintains that, although we are born with an instinct for the spiritual, this instinct needs to be developed like any other natural sense, such as an appreciation of poetry or great music. He sees the cultivation of the spiritual sense as a parental and educational duty in order to enable a child to grow to maturity. The new breed of aggressive atheists, he says, have not had this spiritual sense developed and so they are handicapped in their understanding and appreciation of a vital part of life.[7]

Markham illustrates this with the well-known optical illusion of a picture which can be seen as a young girl looking away from the viewer or an old woman facing us. With a bit of work, one can see both. Sometimes we may fall back into the atheists' problem of only being able to see one side of the picture of life. We lose 'sight' of God; we fail to recognize God's presence in the everyday fabric of life, nature, relationships and events, and God becomes increasingly unreal. The answer is to re-learn the sacred art of seeing.

The novelist Jeanette Winterson said:

> You find manifestations of God everywhere ... So the obvious places where God is to be found – in the synagogues or in the churches, even in the scrolls of the law – are not where God is found. God is found among the ordinary people – at sea, on boats, in the market place, with the whores, with the sinners – so that God is fugitive from our authority. We try and contain God and God always says: 'I'm not here, I'm somewhere else.'[8]

That somewhere else is the ordinary, where God's presence waits to be unveiled (which is what 'revelation' actually means).

Perhaps the most important skill here is to recognize the presence of God within our own lives. The goal of our lives spiritually is union with God, 'mutual indwelling', but we don't know where to find him. That was the experience of the disciples in the days after the resurrection. They were full of hope and desire, having encountered the risen Christ, but they were missing something vital and so they were rooted to the spot, that spot being the upper room in Jerusalem. They had their memories, and now they had had a bewildering few weeks with Jesus popping up here and there, but what were they to do? They must have forgotten the promise, the great, golden, glorious promise that Jesus had given them at their last meal together. The life-changing, world-turning, spine-tingling promise of Jesus, 'I will ask the Father, and he will give you another Advocate, to be with you for ever. This is the Spirit . . . he abides with you, *and he will be in you*' (John 14.16–17).

Bingo! That's what we need – the Spirit of Jesus to be *in us*. Instead of pursuing God and relentlessly asking God for a sign, instead of longing for some external proof ('Yes, I'm sure I felt strangely warmed last Tuesday at 8.30, but then again it could have been those two glasses of red wine'), instead of all that, Jesus is saying, '*I will be in you.*' Instead of worrying about our spiritual temperature, we can relax, let the Spirit breathe within us, and let Jesus work from the inside out. The New Testament is quite clear on this. 'Test yourselves. Do you not realize that *Jesus Christ is in you*?' (2 Cor. 13.5). 'God chose to make known how great . . . are the riches of the glory of this mystery, *which is Christ in you*, the hope of glory' (Col. 1.27).

I once went on an eight-day Ignatian retreat where my guide was an 80-year-old Jesuit priest. Despite being closely modelled on Bilbo Baggins, he went straight to the heart of what I needed on the very first day. 'Let Christ ease his way into your life,' he said, 'and meditate on Paul's astonishing assertion in Galatians chapter 2 that "It is no longer I who live, but Christ who lives in me."' Of course! That's where God is to be found. As a Christian it's no longer me who reigns supreme in my life, standing ridiculously on my little dung-hill of dignity. It's Christ, no less, who lives in me, in you, in us. That isn't to say anything about our goodness or worthiness, but Christ has a home, and it's *in us*. It was pure liberation for me to encounter that deep truth afresh.

Jesus says of the Spirit, 'You know him, because he abides with you, and he will be in you.' And then, in one of the loveliest promises of the New Testament, he says, 'My Father and I will come to you *and make our home with you*' (John 14.17, and cf. v. 23). Home. We know what that's like (for most people). We come back from holiday, pick up the letters from the floor, climb wearily up the stairs and fling the suitcase on the bed. We're back. It's home. And Jesus dares to say that he wants to make his 'home' in our lives.

I've already quoted Martin Laird, 'God does not know how to be absent.' You might say, God is *never not present* in our lives. Can we believe that? It could make all the difference. If I can stay at home and enjoy God's presence – genuinely *be present* to the presence of God – that might be enough to restore my soul. It's the path taken by many others as they have journeyed back to a living faith.

As ever St Augustine has been there before us:

> Late have I loved you, O Beauty ever ancient, ever new, late
> have I loved you! You were within me, but I was outside,
> and it was there that I searched for you. In my unloveliness
> I plunged into the lovely things which you created. You
> were with me, but I was not with you. Created things
> kept me from you; yet if they had not been in you they
> would not have been at all. You called, you shouted,
> and you broke through my deafness. You flashed, you
> shone, and you dispelled my blindness. You breathed your
> fragrance on me; I drew in breath and now I pant for
> you. I have tasted you, now I hunger and thirst for more.
> You touched me, and I burned for your peace.[9]

There was one other problem about locating God unhelpfully that we identified in Chapter 1, and that was the danger in some people of seeing God as 'out to get me'. It's an insidious image of God which usually operates subconsciously but keeps the believer in fear rather than freedom. The corrective from Christian theology was simply expressed by Archbishop Michael Ramsey who once wrote: 'God is Christ-like, and in him is no un-Christ-likeness at all.'[10] If Jesus is God's self-portrait, the author of history appearing on stage himself, then it's in that figure that we have the fullest insight into the nature of God. The God we find there is endless in his loving and inexhaustible in his forgiving. Ask Zacchaeus or the woman taken in adultery, the countless people he healed, the women he honoured, the outcasts and social sinners he rehabilitated, the thief on the cross next to him. They all experienced a God who was far from 'out to get them', but rather one who was eternally 'on their side'. That's the answer for us too.

The three theological issues we have been exploring in this section were about the temptation for our ideas of God to be too transcendent, too spectacular or too scary. If we can straighten out our theology many of the barriers to God's presence that we have unintentionally erected may begin to fade away and the clear golden light of God's day may start to warm our memories. Who is this God we purport to seek and whose way we follow? That's the Christian's most urgent question. God waits not to be located as a stranger and in strange places but to be recognized as Friend and Lord in every place, including in the depth of our own lives.

## Faith not as experience but as obedience

In Chapter 1 we looked at the baffling fact that some Christians hardly ever experience anything of God's presence for large parts – even most – of their lives. Mother Teresa was an example, as was a 90-year-old nun I once met. The tough truth is that this experience is more common than we might think. It's commonly called the 'apophatic' way, the way of darkness and waiting and negativity, the end of images and words and feelings, when prayer is simply hunkering down in the darkness. The contrast is between this way and the 'cataphatic' way which is full of words, concepts and images. This is the way of knowing as opposed to the way of unknowing, the way of light as opposed to the way of darkness. Richard Rohr speaks of the difference between the sun's light and the moon's light. 'The lunar light is much more subtle, filtered and indirect, and sometimes, in that sense, more clarifying and less threatening. The solar light can sometimes be too bright, and so clear that it actually obscures or blinds you.' He maintains that:

> Jesus is much more of a 'lunar' teacher, patient with darkness and growth. Jesus says himself: 'The seed is sprouting and growing but we do not know how' (Mark 4.27). He seems to be willing to live with such not-knowing, surely

82

representing the cosmic patience and sure control of God. When you know you are finally in charge you do not have to nail everything down along the way.[11]

The metaphors of the cataphatic way which most of us take are those of light, vision and mountain tops. The metaphors of the apophatic way are those of the cave, the desert, exile and darkness. The tradition of the mountain is about presence; the tradition of the desert is about absence. It was to the desert that hundreds of monks went from the early fourth century to escape the certainties of the newly appropriated Christianity of Constantine, and the apophatic, contemplative, mystical tradition has constantly resurfaced, quietly breaking through the surface noise of confident Christendom. Examples include the fifth-century Dionysius the Areopagite, the fourteenth-century author of *The Cloud of Unknowing*, and the sixteenth-century St John of the Cross. The latter's teaching on 'the dark night of the soul' has particularly resonated with Christians who have lost contact with God and waited in darkness for long years. His explanation is that when we are very close to God the eye of the soul has to dilate to cope with the fierce light, with the result that all appears dark. Think of a small child being held close to your chest.

It seems that Mother Teresa may have been able to see her own darkness in something like this way. She wrote to a spiritual companion who helped her see her longing for God as a sure sign of his hidden presence:

I can't express in words the gratitude I owe you for your kindness to me. For the first time in years I have come to love the darkness for I believe now that it is part of a very, very small part of Jesus' darkness and pain on earth. You have taught me to accept it [as] a spiritual side of [my] work ... Today I felt a deep joy that Jesus can't go any more through the agony, but that he wants to go through it in me.[12]

Mother Teresa felt a deep sense of release – but it didn't mean that she experienced the presence and love of God herself with any more immediacy. The negative way is still a hard one. The silence of God is still terrible for the believer who wants nothing more than some sign of his nearness.

Moreover, atheists like Philip Pullman regard such interpretations of spiritual darkness as intolerable wriggling by believers unable to face the facts. In his review of Pullman's *The Good Man Jesus and the Scoundrel Christ* Rowan Williams wrote,

> Pullman's Jesus is scathing about 'smart-arse priests' who talk about God's absence really being his presence. Well, yes: Christians use this kind of language. But not to let themselves off lightly; they're arguing that you only get anywhere near the truth when all the easy things to say about God are dismantled – so that your image of God is no longer just a big projection of your self-centred wish-fulfilment fantasies. What's left, then? This is the difficult moment. Either you sense that you are confronting an energy so immense and unconditioned that there are no adequate words for it; or you give up.[13]

That is the existential choice many people face.

One of the lessons we learn from those who habitually find themselves in darkness is that God is answerable to God alone. He is not ours to pressurize or manipulate. Dietrich Bonhoeffer wrote in *Meditating on the Word*:

> If it is I who say where God will be, I will always find there a false God who in some way corresponds to me, is agreeable to me, fits in with my nature. But if it is God who says where he will be ... that place is the cross of Christ.[14]

We have to learn again the importance of letting God be God, and then not to be surprised if he is most recognizable in the dark figure on the cross.

Indeed there is some evidence that, following the Holocaust and the horrific list of twentieth and twenty-first-century tragedies, it is primarily on the cross that today's Western culture is able to meet God. A God who is noisy, confident and full of answers is less acceptable than a 'lunar' God of more nuanced assertions, a God who asks questions and invites an exploration of mystery. The philosopher Peter Rollins in *How (Not) to Speak of God* writes:

> The emerging conversation is demonstrating an ability to stand up and engage in a powerless, space-creating discourse that opens up thinking and offers hints rather than orders. In short, the emerging community must endeavour to be a question rather than an answer and an aroma rather than food ... For too long the Church has been seen as an oasis in the desert – offering water to those who are thirsty. In contrast, the emerging community appears more as a desert in the oasis of life, offering silence, space and desolation amidst the sickly nourishment of Western capitalism.[15]

What then is the answer for those who experience nothing? It seems to be this: what we are called to is simple obedience, not a popular concept today but one due for a comeback. In Gethsemane Jesus asked his three closest friends to 'remain here, and stay awake with me' (Matt. 26.38). That is what he asks of us, whether we then experience his presence or not. Our task is to stay.

Perhaps the apophatic way is due for a new (if quiet) revival.

In this chapter we have tried to see faith in somewhat different ways – not as regulation but as relationship, not as arrival but as quest, not as success but as direction, not as locating God at a distance but as recognizing God in the midst, not as experience but as obedience. Can we re-imagine faith along the lines of a God like that? If so, God might rise again in our lives and become even more glorious.

# 7

## 'Earth's crammed with heaven'

———•◦•———

It was five in the morning and the night had been bitterly cold. But then, at Annapurna base camp in the Himalayas, what could one expect? I had slept in several layers of clothing in a four-seasons sleeping bag with only my nose poking out, but I was still cold and glad to get moving. Dawn was casting a calm light into our wooden hut. I struggled into yet more clothes and icy boots, and then went outside.

It was only a hundred yards up the slope to the moraine we hadn't been able to see the night before when we arrived in the steady snowfall, but I knew this was the vantage point we needed. When I got there I looked up and if I hadn't already been silent in the early dawn I would have been struck dumb. Around me were at least ten peaks which stood over 20,000 feet high (6,100 metres). The distances were disconcerting but these giant sentinels stood guard all around us – not for nothing is it called the Annapurna Sanctuary. The peaks glowed pink in the dawn light and their massive silence was overwhelming. Above all I was awestruck by the scale of these majestic mountains. My idea of a mountain was shaped by the Lake District peaks where Scafell Pike is the highest at just 3,209 feet (978 metres). These around Annapurna were off the scale.

My companion and I were speechless. We looked and looked. We drank in the beauty. And in the profound silence I gave thanks to the Creator. How could I not? Awesome is a distressingly overused word nowadays, but it was for this that the word was intended. When the late actress Dame Sybil Thorndike was a young girl she visited Niagara Falls and wrote to her parents about the experience. She said:

I've seen it. The trouble is I've run out of adjectives. I've used up all the wonderfuls and marvellouses. So take all the wonderfuls and marvellouses, multiply them a hundred times, sing them to the Halleluia Chorus, King of Kings, Lord of Lords, and you'll know something of what I'm feeling.[1]

That's what I felt beneath Annapurna.

I believe that for many people an approach to the divine is made most easily through the natural world. I might like to think that being introduced to the person of Jesus would bring people to their knees, but experience suggests that a walk on the hills or digging in a garden is for many people a surer guide to the geography of God. It may therefore be that when we have lost contact with God in church or in our praying, one of the things not to do is to 'push it' but instead to 'let go' into the wonder of the truly astonishing beauty, complexity and power of nature. This is where Elizabeth Barrett Browning's words ring true for many: 'Earth's crammed with heaven, and every common bush afire with God, but only he who sees, takes off his shoes.'[2]

I hesitate to write this but when Dorothy Frances Gurney wrote, 'One is nearer God's heart in a garden than anywhere else on earth,' for many people that is exactly right. It may be sentimental, but it may also be accurate. My wife is much moved by the process of gardening. As I watch her (note the verb!) and listen to her speak about the effect it has on her, I recognize a connectedness with creation that is deeply spiritual. She once wrote:

When we moved to Gateshead I discovered that gardening was the joy of my life. I would come home from a full day at work, put on my jeans and dig. Nothing beats it. I get withdrawal symptoms if I have to go for a week without digging. There's a deeper force at work in a gardener's soul, though, than just the joy of raising healthy plants. A garden is where

God's creativity and ours enmesh, where we can be part of his processes and work alongside the divine life-giver. To work with the soil and feel its rich rhythms is to share in God's love of this world in a unique way. I love the image of Jesus as a gardener too. Jesus the gardener entered fully into our world with his sleeves rolled up and dirt under his fingernails. That's the sort of God I want – Alleluia!

The danger is that the Church has tried to monopolize spiritual experience and package it in suitable ecclesiastical wrapping paper (plain or multi-coloured according to taste), but more people probably encounter God in the mountains, in gardens, in deserts, by the sea, in brilliant sunsets and hushed silver dawns than in Morning Prayer and Evensong, even in their most up-to-date *Common Worship* format. The natural world could be the way back for many whose faith has faded under the assault of too much institutional religion.

### *Attentiveness*

The key attitude that we need to bring to the experiences we're thinking about is attentiveness. In a multi-sensory culture we are easily distracted by the bright and shiny things, the style of a new product from Apple, the glamour of celebrities, the daring of the latest edgy film. But there is a deeper and older wisdom which recognizes that while much forgettable trivia spins away, the beauty and elegance of created things has longer-lasting substance. What we need to bring to created things is the quality of attentiveness. As Martin Luther said: 'If you could understand one grain of wheat you would die of wonder.'

When I find myself overwhelmed with work and slowing down into inefficiency or 'poor me' martyrdom, it's the garden that I resort to. I wander round, trying to slow down to the speed of nature, looking into the open heart of a radiant tulip, noting the play of light and colour which nature achieves so effortlessly, falling under the spell of the birdsong I usually filter out of my hearing. The secret is to slow down and look, smell, touch, listen. More often than not when we do this we're likely to experience what the novelist A. S. Byatt referred to as the 'designed poetry' of nature's genius. We respond to the non-negotiable essence of each created thing, what G. K. Chesterton called the 'startling wetness of water . . . the fieriness of fire, the steeliness of steel, the unutterable muddiness of mud'.[3]

Gerard Manley Hopkins, that extraordinary Roman Catholic priest and poet, wrote of our encounter with nature:

> All things therefore are charged with love,
> are charged with God,
> and if we know how to touch them,
> give off sparks and take fire,
> yield drops and flow,
> ring and tell of him.[4]

'All things . . . give off sparks and take fire' if we are receptive and attentive – 'if we know how to touch them'. It's the touching and looking that we bring to the experience, a touching and attentiveness that is intentional and patient. If we really want to return to an awareness of God, surely that isn't too much to ask?

## Wonder and silence

A few years ago I went on a pilgrimage through the Sinai desert to the holy mountain where God, by tradition, disclosed himself to Moses. The goal was important, but not as much as the journey – a week trekking through the wild rocky desert out of sight of any twenty-first-century accretions. It was hot during the day, over 30C, but, when the buffeting winds of dusk had passed, it became freezing cold at night as we slept under the stars, watching the astonishing light-show of the galaxies above. There was frost on our sleeping bags in the morning. As we got going on our trek, we determined to spend the first two hours of the

day walking in complete silence, drinking in the profound otherness of the desert. It was magical. We walked in the shadow of
the people of Israel, searching for their new home. We walked
in the shadow of the desert fathers, going out into the wild
places to face their demons. We walked in the shadow of Jesus,
taking to the desert to have it out with the devil. We walked in
our own shadow, examining our life journeys, our motivations,
our vulnerabilities. The desert was full of wonder and silence.

It is often in places of fragility and vulnerability that our
journey back to an awareness of God begins. When we have
lost our spiritual bearings it may be that we should have recourse
to some form of desert. When everything else is stripped away
and it's just you, nature and God, nature may well respond
and reveal the secrets of her Creator. The ancient Oxyrynchus
papyrus has a passage, 'Lift up the stone and you will find me;
cleave the wood and I am there. He that wonders shall reign.'
If we open ourselves to wonder at the sheer 'is-ness' of things
we may well begin to discover what Shakespeare meant when
he wrote that there are 'tongues in trees, books in the running
brooks, sermons in stones, and good in everything'.

Of course it isn't necessary to travel as far as the Sinai desert
to discover the wonder and simplicity that nature teaches. It's
on the doorstep of everyone's life. The trick is to exercise the
gentle discipline necessary to explore this open road to God.

## Simple disciplines

If I am right there's no need for superhuman effort to hunt
God down in this approach to rediscovering faith. Nor does it
require suspension of disbelief or a renewed encounter with
the religious systems that may have hurt us. It requires simply
the grace of holy attentiveness. I add the adjective 'holy' because
there is a profound holiness in the business of attending to the
other, whether that 'other' be a glorious rose or a glorious person.
When we listen attentively to another person telling us things

of significance in their life we are standing on sacred ground. Our empathy, eye-contact and focused following of their story is a priceless gift, given rarely enough in our self-centred and narcissistic culture. A 2010 report from the University of Michigan Institute for Social Research found that, 'College kids today are about 40% lower in empathy than their counterparts of twenty or thirty years ago.' Another analysis concluded, 'Many people see the current group of college students, sometimes called "Generation Me", as one of the most self-centred, narcissistic, competitive, confident and individualistic in recent history.'[5]

Against this waning of empathy, people of faith practise the art of holy attentiveness both to other people and to the created world. The latter helps the former. As we learn to stand outside ourselves and appreciate something else for all that it is, so we may become more aware of the realities of another person's life. Here are some simple ways to practise holy attentiveness:

- Set out to enjoy creation. Look for beauty. Be positive about the portion of God's creation to which you have access, whether it be a glorious view from a kitchen window or a few plants in a window box. G. K. Chesterton wrote, 'There is but one sin: to call a green leaf grey.'[6]
- Get your feet off carpet and concrete as often as you can. To feel the good earth beneath our feet is at once very healing and also a reminder that in constructing a civilization we have often lost an awareness of the deeper currents and energies of God's creation.
- Engage with detail in creation. Contemplate, wonder, give thanks. It's fascinating to watch a small child interact with a very small discovery in a garden path or a flower border. There's enough miracle in that tiny patch of ground to keep a child entranced. Whatever happened to that quality of wonder in us? Let me give an example. Annie Dillard is an American writer who is exquisitely aware of details. In her book *Pilgrim at Tinker Creek* she writes of encountering a butterfly:

It is easy to coax an exhausted butterfly onto your finger. I saw a monarch walking across a gas station lot; it was walking south. I placed my index finger in its path, and it clambered aboard and let me lift it to my face. Its wings were faded but unmarked by hazard; a veneer of velvet caught the light and hinted at the frailest depth of lapped scales. It was a male; his legs clutching my finger were short and atrophied; they clasped my finger with a spread fragility, a fineness as of some low note of emotion or pure strain of spirit, scarcely perceived. And I knew that those feet were actually tasting me, sipping with sensitive organs the vapour of my finger's skin: butterflies taste with their feet. All the time he held me, he opened and closed his glorious wings, senselessly, as if sighing.[7]

The description of that encounter goes on for another full page. This was just an exhausted butterfly 'walking south', but it evoked a depth of observation and attention that is enviable to those of us who would have wandered innocently by. Engage with detail.

- As you walk the dog or go to the local shops, try to walk more slowly (it will be hard). And as you walk, look, smell, touch, listen. A whole world of new sensory experiences will open up which are usually screened out by our distraction and haste. Be aware that this ability to attend to nature will easily fade unless encouraged. William Blake observed, 'The tree which moves some to tears of joy is, in the eyes of others, only a green thing which stands in the way.'[8] Developers beware!
- Try to spend time by running water, be it a stream, a fountain or a rocky shore line. Running water is astonishing in its endless, patterned inventiveness. One writer has observed:

The streaming of water around rock is one of the most complex motions of which human beings are aware. The change from a laminar, more or less uniform flow to turbulent flow around a single rock is so abstruse a transition mathematically that even the most sophisticated computer cannot make it through to a satisfactory description.[9]

Running water never ceases to amaze me by its patience. It never takes no for an answer, always finding a way through obstructions, and thereby teaching me about the patient persuasion of divine love. It never repeats itself and yet it keeps its innovations within recognizable patterns, again teaching me about the way God searches out the possibilities latent in his world and his people, while respecting their intrinsic limitations. Running water takes me back to Scripture and its evocative use of the image of water. The psalms name the problem we're exploring: 'As a deer longs for flowing streams, so my soul longs for you, O God. My soul thirsts for God, for the living God. When shall I come and behold the face of God?' (Ps. 42.1–2) But there is hope: 'Waters shall break forth in the wilderness, and streams in the desert; the burning sand shall become a pool, and the thirsty ground springs of water' (Isa. 35.6–7). And Jesus too: 'The water that I will give will become in them a spring of water gushing up to eternal life' (John 4.14). The metaphor of running, living water is a powerful descriptor and a healing image for many.

- Have you thought of putting three conkers in your coat pocket in the autumn? They can help us to pray, focusing our prayers on God as Father, Son or Holy Spirit. They also represent the living world of which we are a part and for which we have a responsibility of care and protection.
- My wife would say 'Get your hands dirty in the soil.' I take her word for it, but (apparently) this facilitates a deep engagement with the natural world out of which all life comes. It makes life tangible and tactile. It heals; it restores; it may even forgive. Martin Luther said, 'In every created thing there is the forgiveness of sins.'

- I can, however, personally vouch for the wonder of a newborn child. On the day I'm writing this our younger daughter has produced a 6lb 6 oz baby who is uniquely miraculous. I hold in awe the tiny hand of a newborn child and am amazed at the detail of those little fingers, clinging boldly to my own. Inside that child are countless miles of wiring and the simultaneous firing of millions of synapses as this little scrap of humanity embarks on life. It's a miracle of the first order and brings the strongest of us to gentleness and tears.

St Augustine wrote:

Some people, in order to discover God, read books. But there is a great book: the very nature of created things. Look above you! Look below you! Note it. Read it. God, whom you want to discover, never wrote that book with ink. Instead He set before your eyes the things that He had made. Can you ask for a louder voice than that? Why, heaven and earth shout to you, 'God made me!'[10]

Many people are sensitive to the voice of nature when the voice of God in Scripture or in church has grown dim. It won't be for everybody. A tree may still be 'only a green thing which stands in the way'. Nevertheless, here in the book of nature may be one key to returning to a living faith through re-turning – turning again – to the familiarity and strangeness of nature and encountering its exotic voice. As we give natural things the dignity of our attention, we might find that God's reassuring presence steals quietly back over our parched spiritual landscape.

There is a further possibility when we open ourselves to wonder. Wonder can begin to arouse the possibility of the divine, but the theologian Michael Paul Gallagher writes that we need to 'awaken the sleeping beauty of our wonder so that we can be more ready for the greater wonder that is Jesus Christ'.[11]

And in terms of faith, that would truly be like winning Olympic gold.

# 8

## 'Yes' as a way of life

The American Franciscan Richard Rohr is fond of saying that God comes to us disguised as life. In other words, God is not to be encountered in the margins of our experience, but in the centre, and especially wherever we encounter richness of life. The mistaken relegation of God to places where strange things happen on the edges of normality has displaced him from the heart of human experience, with considerable collateral damage to people's awareness of God as the source and centre of every aspect of life lived fully and well.

It has been said that life is a chain of unrequited desires: men want women, women want children, and children want hamsters. But all of us want that elusive experience we call 'Life'. Jesus said that his whole purpose had been to give us life in abundance (John 10.10). He didn't say he intended to make us religious or even to make us moral. He said he had come to give us life itself and life to the full. So maybe it's through the particular doorway of 'life' that we might begin a journey back to the awareness of God if we've somehow lost him on the way. The category of religion may have become too burdensome, but the category of 'life' might be more rewarding.

### Choose life

A possible way back to faith, then, may be intentionally to choose the way of 'life' wherever that is to be found. At some point we're likely to bump into God. And if 'the earth is the LORD's and all that is in it' (Ps. 24.1) then this experience of life doesn't have to be religious in the conventional sense. Bel Mooney researched and introduced a radio series of conversations with those she called 'Devout Sceptics' and she summed up her experience like this: 'Four elements of secular life today can lead to glimmerings of the divine: scientific knowledge, awareness of the environment, the wide availability of the arts, and the psychological study of human nature.'[1] None of those is specifically religious. The presence of the divine is more subtly pervasive in the whole warp and weft of life.

So when do we find life overflowing like the warm sun on a Mediterranean morning? When do we feel completely fulfilled and at peace with the world? When do we know the simple joy that makes the heart rise up and emerge as a smile? This experience of abundance is one that we may seek out by pursuing some activity or hobby we know we'll enjoy. The diversity of human enthusiasms is a constant source of delight to me. Across the country people come home from work and turn to thousands of hobbies of which I have no understanding at all – wonderful! Alternatively, the experience of joy may come upon us unexpectantly and even in the most unlikely places. Etty Hillesum was a young Dutch Jew who went (voluntarily – a longer story) into a concentration camp in the Second World War and died in Auschwitz in 1943, aged 28. She wrote in her diary:

> The misery here is quite terrible and yet, late at night when the day has slunk away into the depths behind me, I often walk with a spring in my step along the barbed wire and then time and again it soars straight from my heart – I can't help it, that's just the way it is, like some elemental force – the feeling that life is glorious and magnificent, and that one day we shall be building a whole new world. Against every new outrage and every fresh horror we shall put up one more piece of love and goodness, drawing strength from within ourselves.[2]

Life is irrepressible. It bubbles up within us and reminds us that all is never lost. But that flow of life within us may also be stained with darker colours and the task then becomes one of sorting out the creative and destructive elements that compete for our attention, and then choosing the creative, choosing life. That was the call of God to the Israelites when he was reminding them yet again in their desert wanderings that he was with them and all would be well, but only if they chose life instead of death. 'I have set before you life and death, blessings and curses. Choose life so that you and your descendants may live' (Deut. 30.19). It's a fundamental choice and it has far-reaching consequences. Chosen well, this path can lead us to recognize the presence of God in the entire fabric of life. 'Omitted,' says Shakespeare, 'all the voyage of their life is bound in shallows and in misery' (*Julius Caesar*, IV. iii. 218–19). Etty Hillesum chose life by putting 'one more piece of love and goodness' against 'every new outrage and every fresh horror'.

Denis Potter the playwright was interviewed by Melvyn Bragg shortly before he died of cancer in 1994. He agreed that there were many things he could no longer do but, he said,

> I can celebrate life! Below my window there's an apple tree in blossom. It's white. And looking at it – instead of saying 'Oh that's a nice blossom,' – now, looking at it through the window, I see the whitest, frothiest, blossomest blossom that there ever could be. The nowness of everything is absolutely wondrous. If you see the present tense – boy, do you see it, and boy, do you celebrate it![3]

One can say 'yes' to life at any time and place, and the secret is so often to live in the present miraculous moment.

We come back, therefore, to the search for authenticity in religious faith. It isn't the religion that matters. All religion does is offer a vehicle in which faith can travel and, in particular, can be handed on from generations past to generations present.

The words of the theologian/poet John V. Taylor have often resonated strongly with me at this point:

> It has long been my conviction that God is not hugely concerned as to whether we are religious or not. What matters to God, and matters supremely, is whether we are alive or not. If your religion brings you more fully to life, God will be in it; but if your religion inhibits your capacity for life or makes you run away from it, you may be sure God is against it, just as Jesus was.[4]

We are alive in Taylor's terms when we watch the sun rise in streaks of gold over a still sea, when we stumble, exhilarated, to the final summit of the mountain, when we listen to music so beautiful we silently weep, when we crack some intellectual puzzle that we've been working on for ages, or when we fall in love and we've never known life could be so clear and colourful. And if these examples are too extreme, then turn down the colour a little and find your own equivalents; we all have them.

God, I believe, revels in all of this. God is not a narrow-minded, repressive deity fingering the red card he wants to brandish at his failing followers. God is a huge, all-embracing giver and sustainer of life, committed to the flourishing and happiness of his people. Both individuals and religious movements can be crudely divided into those that emphasize the Fall and the failings of humankind, and those that emphasize the possibilities of redemption and hope. The one is addicted to saying 'no', the other to saying a forgiving 'yes'. I'm clear that, as Paul says, 'in him [Christ] it is always "Yes." For in him every one of God's promises is a "Yes"' (2 Cor.1.19–20).

It follows that what matters to God is not some optional activity we call religion, but life itself, all of it – science and art and politics and prison reform and peace movements, and why we keep destroying the planet and why we spend so much on what we ironically call 'defence' and why England teams are so fragile and why contemporary films are so full of theological questions, and so on. God's specialist subject is Life.

And here, maybe, is the crunch – it's possible to get it wrong, to choose death by mistakenly thinking it's life. Many things look like life, with the glitz and glamour sold to us by a thousand adverts, and the power and influence we imagine goes with top jobs and high salaries. However, all that glisters is not always gold, and the environments such people inhabit could be characterized by short cuts and short honesty, where ethics are seen as weakness and people are treated as pawns. Choosing life is rather more subtle than that. So it's probably true that our wedding won't feature in *Hello!* magazine; our lottery number will never come up; we won't make it on to a reality TV show. But there are much more significant characteristics of this 'abundant life'. Choosing life means something like choosing quality, not quantity; choosing virtue, not expediency; choosing character, not consumerism; choosing humility, not hubris, choosing courage, not the siren song of the crowd; choosing faith, not the convenient agnosticism of the age, and so on. It's about going the long road with lasting values, and relishing the journey. Above all, it's about love as a way of life.

## Where does 'life' crop up?

People find life in all sorts of places that are quite implausible to me. They are obsessive about golf or fishing or war games or water lilies or London buses or train timetables or Henry VIII or sailing. I like the observation about sailing I once read, that the best way for beginners to get a taste for it is to stand under a cold shower tearing up £20 notes. Steve Wright also once observed that there's a fine line between fishing and just standing on the shore like an idiot. How can grown-up people commit themselves wholeheartedly to the World Welly Throwing Competition held in South Island, New Zealand? Or how can mature adults spend their lives waiting for Bonnie Prince

Charlie's heir to return to take the Scottish throne? However, I'm fascinated by the enthusiasm and passion that all these interests and hobbies generate. When I listen to such passion I catch a glimpse of whole other worlds of which I have no knowledge. How is it possible to have a monthly magazine devoted simply to catching trout? To my untutored mind when you've caught a trout, you've caught a trout. But there is clearly an entire trout universe out there of which I am criminally ignorant.

The point about these worlds of passionate interest and commitment is that they are life-giving to the participants. However they got into these extraordinary hobbies, they are obviously finding in them both absorbing purpose and deep satisfaction and, I believe, they are touching the hem of God's delight as they explore the rich possibilities of God's world. For those who are seeking a route back to an awareness of God it might be that pondering the pleasure we find in our hobbies, interests and commitments might give us a hook to hang on to. The simple connection between these hobbies and our faith journey might perhaps be made by reflecting on just how incredibly interesting life is, how full of fascination and diversity – and how unlikely it all is. What or who is the source of such richness? Are we doomed to see all this as sheer cosmic accident, something glorious coming out of nothing? Is there no hint of a wonderfully imaginative, and indeed playful, Mind?

People find life-at-depth in all sorts of wonderfully unlikely places. I know and admire a woman who looks after 800 goats and knows them all by name. I know bee-keepers for whom death by stinging is obviously not a problem. I've watched people re-enacting battles with ferocious intent and simply wondered 'Why?' I know someone whose hobby was admitted, when pushed, to be lighthouses, alive or dead. I know several people whose hobby is wine-tasting (getting warmer) and many more who are obsessed with cricket (ah – we've arrived!). In the film *Billy Elliott*, Billy is at an audition for a ballet school in

London. Out of his cultural depth, Billy hasn't done well and is about to be sent away when one of the assessors suddenly asks him, 'Billy, what do you feel when you dance?' There's a silence while Billy tries to find the words. 'Electricity,' he says at last, 'it's like electricity.' He gets in.

This is God's world, and human inventiveness and creativity reflect the irrepressible creativity of God, in whose image we are made. To be creative and to turn towards life is the common experience of every human being, unless and until they are wounded on the way. We are most human when we create, and most divine.

## This sporting life

Anyone who, like me, has been a supporter of Blackpool football club over the last few decades has been acquainted with pain. At the time of writing, the pain has at last been relieved by promotion to the Premiership, but the scars go deep. Football, like any sport, can deliver encouragement and despair in mountainous quantities. The reason for that is that sport (and let's take football as an example) is not just, as J. B. Priestley once observed, 'conflict and art', it's also big business and – increasingly – religion. All the elements are there: the players are gods, the ground is the temple, the stands are the pews, the worship is sung with arms outstretched to heaven. Advertising plays to the same theme – 'Come and worship at Anfield this Sunday'. The legendary manager of Liverpool, Bill Shankly, once famously remarked: 'Some people think football is a matter of life and death. I can assure them it's much more serious than that.'

Peter Wilcox remarks in *Praying for England*: 'Football achieves a quasi-religious status in British society because of its capacity to provide art, drama, a moral framework and, crucially, belonging.'[5] The art lies in the 'moments of acrobatic, balletic skill, moments when a player exhibits such speed and power, ball control and balance that spectators experience a moment of shared ecstasy'. The drama lies in the familiar scripts – matches that are 'David and Goliath' fixtures, 'messiahs' coming to the rescue, 'Judas' returning to a club he's left, 'resurrection' when a team snatches an unlikely victory. Moreover, grown men embrace complete strangers or weep without embarrassment, depending on the situation. It's all highly theatrical. The moral framework of football is always being tested but that's the nature of moral frameworks. And the final element that Wilcox mentions – belonging – is seen in the fierce loyalty and sense of identity that resides in the average supporter (even of Blackpool). When Bobby Robson became manager of Newcastle he said, 'If you cut me, I bleed black and white' (the Newcastle colours).

Sport, then, is easily seen as an 'alternative religion', particularly in poorer communities and working-class estates where the Church makes little headway. However, seen in the context of the argument of this chapter, that God affirms 'life' wherever it emerges in someone's experience, this devotion to sport can be re-imagined as part of God's great 'yes' to life ('In him it is always yes'). Is there a way of working backwards from this apparently secular passion to an awareness of the God who says 'yes'? Perhaps there is such a route when we reflect on the nature of the God we think we believe in. If our God is so small that he resides chiefly in church activities (and therefore mainly for females over 50), then we will indeed see football primarily as an alternative, competing route to the enjoyment of life. But if we can re-imagine God as truly the giver and preserver of life in all its parts, we may be able to encounter God again as immeasurably larger and more creative than we ever imagined. In that way perhaps passion for sport can lead us back to passion for God.

## The arts

In the book that Bel Mooney wrote out of her radio conversations, *Devout Sceptics*, she ventured to say, 'I have no doubt that agnostics like myself tiptoe towards the deity while listening to music. It is easy to decry the worst excesses of popular culture; the fact remains that Art has the power to make the universe shiver.[6] It is this shivering that very large numbers of people experience in the presence of great music, painting, theatre, literature, poetry, film and the like. The arts have a power to get under the skin, to get past our usual filters of self-censorship, and to interrogate our thoughts, our emotions and sometimes even our world-view. D. H. Lawrence said, 'I always feel as if I stood naked for the fire of Almighty God to go through me – and it's rather an awful feeling. One has to be so terribly religious to be an artist.'[7]

In his book *Real Presences* George Steiner makes the case for the artistic response leading to the reality of the transcendent. He states his thesis like this: 'I will put forward the argument that the experience of aesthetic meaning, in particular that of literature, of the arts, of musical form, infers the necessary possibility of this "real presence" [of God]'.[8] Great art comes from divine reality, he maintains.

> There is aesthetic creation because there is creation ... I take the aesthetic act, the conceiving and bringing into being of that which, very precisely, could not have been conceived or brought into being, to be an *imitation*, a replication on its own scale, of the inaccessible first *fiat* (the Big Bang of the new cosmologies).

So, says Professor Ian Markham, Dean of Virginia Theological Seminary, 'The miracle of Mozart's *Don Giovanni* (the capacity to create inspirational music from nothing) is a human echo of the divine achievement of creating cosmos out of nothing.'[9]

However, more germane to our own concern is not where artistic inspiration comes from but how we, bemused seekers after God, encounter God through the arts. The answer, both for Steiner and for Markham, is that we can cultivate our spiritual senses in the same way that we cultivate other senses in order fully to appreciate and enjoy the world. From baby-hood on, we learn how to see more accurately, and how to interpret what we see. We enjoy educating our taste buds (back to wine-tasting again). We learn the many meanings of sounds, from bird songs to human arias. Similarly we will be deficient in our skills for living and appreciating life if we don't develop our spiritual senses. These are the pointers to the transcendent that we get from the experience of love and the enjoyment of the arts – those special encounters with music, painting, literature and poetry that seem to liberate the soul and let it fly. Recently I went to a concert which included Tchaikovsky's 5th Symphony, in which the exuberance of the conductor was intoxicating both for the orchestra and for this innocent member of the audience. How could I not smile like a fool? I was in the presence of more joy than I could easily contain. It might be a short step for some to move from joy in the arts to joy in the divine Artist.

### 'Come alive'

The encounter with life is an encounter with God. The trick is to recognize the fact. Sometimes we lose contact with God because we have lost the ability to see deeply enough. Our spiritual antennae have rusted up and we see the signs without getting the meaning. The contention of this chapter is that it's possible to re-engage with our spiritual journey when we share God's delight in life and track our pleasure back to its source. We all start with a (God-given) drive towards life. We foster the most astonishing variety of enthusiasms in our hobbies, interests and commitments, and we share a desire to come alive as fully as possible in the years we have left on this spinning planet. The rock star Sting from the group The Police was asked in an interview what he was looking forward to, now he had achieved so much. He answered:

The ride. The curiosity of what happens next. When I left teaching they said, 'If you leave now you will lose your pension,' and I could see myself at 58 as a deputy head with a pension in the offing, and that's why I left. I didn't want to see the future. I wanted to spin the wheel, and I'm glad to have spun that wheel a few times.[10]

We all have that desire to 'spin the wheel', to fill life to the brim and not simply to have visited this world as a passing tourist. As we give ourselves to the passions we all have in one area or another perhaps we might recognize the smiling presence of the Giver of life. Perhaps we might celebrate the sheer, magnificent abundance of life and smile back. Perhaps the pilot light of faith might catch fire again and eventually the spiritual boiler might burn with hope. We can hope so.

One last thing: it's the experience of millions of people that the key to this 'coming alive' rests with that man, Jesus, who promised that his main purpose in coming was that we might have life and have it abundantly. That's certainly my experience and I've written about it elsewhere. In the Middle Ages death was often portrayed as a skeleton with a scythe, with the implication that when you met death your life blood drained away and you were finished. However, with Jesus it's the diametric opposite – when you meet him you meet life in all it's fullness. It's the kiss of life. So John V. Taylor could give this invitation in a series of talks at Oxford University:

> Come alive to the presence of Jesus Christ and the vast, embracing joy of God. Come alive towards the richness of your experience; come alive towards other people; come alive to the glory and tragedy of the world; come alive to the reality of yourself; come alive to your responsibility to society; above all, come alive to the scriptures and the life of prayer.[11]

Sounds good to me. Choose life!

# 9

## *Awakening the sleeping giant*

One way of describing contemporary Westerners is that we are a culture of sleepwalkers. We go through so much of life unaware of what's happening nearby. If only we could recognize the reality and possibilities of the present moment we might be much more alive to ourselves and to God.

A violinist once went busking for 45 minutes. In that time about 2,000 people went past him. He played some very demanding music on what looked like a well-loved instrument. Some people put money in the violin case on the ground in front of him, but hardly any checked their stride, let alone stopped to listen. Most people hurried past, eyes averted. At the end of the time the violinist had collected 32 dollars. That evening the violinist played at the best concert hall in the city. The tickets were extremely expensive. He used the same instrument as in the morning, valued at about three and a half million dollars. He played the same highly demanding music as he'd played in the subway. His name was Joshua Bell and he was one of the most accomplished violinists in the world.

If we can miss one of the greatest musicians playing one of the most difficult pieces of music with one of the most valuable instruments, might we not be missing much else of importance as we hurry through life with our eyes on the pavement? There is in each of us a huge potential to recognize and respond to the transcendent in our midst, but so often we are half asleep. We blunder through life like today's commuters lost in the world of their headphones, focused only on getting to their destinations safe in their own cocoons, unaware of the fascinating world of sounds and sensations going on around them.

If we have lost track of God, perhaps we have let ourselves slip into this somnolent state and lost sight of the immediacy and richness of the present moment. Perhaps we've forgotten the potential that lies within us and settled for a mundane, half-bored existence. Can we awaken the sleeping giant?

## *Slowing down*

If we are to reconnect with God our first step may well need to be to slow down. Speed is much over-valued in our culture. We want instant access to everything, instant credit, instant answers, ultra-fast internet connection, speed-dating, a quicky divorce. To go slowly is to lose. To ponder is to watch the winner powering his way past us. Try driving slowly on a motorway or walking at a leisurely pace down the platform at Paddington station. The deeper fear is that if we slow down in a liquid culture we'll sink and probably drown. The only way to avoid drowning is to skim over the surface. Don't stop to ask awkward questions like: Why are we doing this? Do we know where we're going? Could we be doing this differently? Is everybody happy?

Bishop Stephen Cottrell wrote a very popular little book with the wonderfully enigmatic title, *Do Nothing to Change Your Life*. He dared to ask those questions and suggested that slowing down was actually essential to our happiness and sanity. He told of the occasion when he suddenly had a wild idea when he stood up to speak at a secondary school assembly. He reminded the pupils that since they got up they'd probably been surrounded by noise and frenetic activity. So he suggested that they might like to try another way and do something different for one minute each day in Lent. He said it would change their life.

I then picked up a chair, placed it in the centre of the stage, and slowly and carefully sat down upon it, with my feet slightly apart, and with my back straight and with my hands resting gently on my knees. And for a minute I sat still. I didn't say anything, and I didn't do anything. I wasn't even consciously praying. I was just sitting there. And I breathed deeply, and I thought about my breathing. And when I reckoned the minute was over, I stood up. But before I could say my next bit there was a huge, spontaneous round of applause.[1]

Even the fast-moving young recognize that speed can be a snare and a delusion. Unless we learn to walk at three miles an hour we won't easily walk with God or recognize God's presence. We'll have rushed past the God we long for. God was busking in the subway and we tossed him some coins as we sped past. God's speed is a human speed, thoughtful and reflective, the speed of friendship.

The speed we choose is surely something to adapt wisely to circumstances, sometimes fast (a fire alarm), sometimes slow (exploring the garden with my two-year-old grandchild). No one says to a conductor that if he'd played that Beethoven symphony at twice the speed he could have finished the concert in half the time. Make no mistake, slowing down is undoubtedly counter-cultural and distinctly hard to maintain. Nevertheless, at a deep level we know, like those secondary school pupils, that slowing down is essential to our humanity. The sleeping giant within us will stay asleep unless he has opportunity to notice the depth and mystery of what lies before his half-closed eyes. Slowing down allows us to see.

What can we do? A simple thing is to pause between tasks. There's no iron rule that we have to start our next task immediately we've finished the previous one. We could pause and enjoy the moment, the room, the view through the window, the pleasure of finishing the last task. It would represent a symbolic victory for the present moment. Another simple thing I try to do (and very often fail) is to pray for the recipient of a letter or card I'm just signing, or pray for the person to whom I've been talking when I put the phone down. It's not difficult and it might make all the difference in the world. Other things? Keep to the speed limit, without pushing it to the edge where you might get caught. Savour meals rather than treating them as a fuel stop, and if that means opening a bottle of wine, why not? Don't be driven by your email, but answer it when *you* want to. Don't turn the radio on the moment you hit the bathroom. Make sure there are a few minutes of every day when you are in silence. Cook slowly (and better than me), stirring the pan and pondering. Wash up with others rather than using the dishwasher.

Note that these simple actions are not overtly religious, but they appeal to spiritual needs for space and reflection which are common to all human beings. The crossover between religious spirituality and what some see as ordinary human spirituality is easily achieved. (Christians would say this is because so-called religious spirituality is always about what is true for all humankind, not just a narrow option for those who like to indulge in esoteric practices.) Paul Walker, a hospital chaplain in the north-east of England, runs retreats for NHS staff as part of a wider business case on wellbeing. He introduces participants to three basic meditation techniques: mindfulness, to experience the present moment; visualization, to use the imagination in meditation; and the Ignatian 'Examen', to reflect on the day, noting what gives consolation and what gives desolation. They are offered space to walk and think, time to share experiences with each other, and the opportunity to have a personal conversation with a member of the chaplaincy team. The feedback has been astonishing with the retreats being given the highest level of satisfaction the NHS Trust has ever recorded in its training.[2] Again we see how important it is in our frenetic, first-past-the-post culture that we take control of our lives and slow down. And this is particularly the case if we are hoping to encounter God afresh, having sped down the road in a cloud of dust that obscured the Divine Hitchhiker and left us unsure where we were going.

These are just examples of a hundred ways we could all slow down. The important thing is that they lead us by waters that are more still than turbulent, and they give us a clue about the hidden depths that await our discovery in every moment and place, if we will but notice. We are actually shaping a more contemplative spirit. And we'll be nicer to know.

## *Creative spirituality*

I have a suspicion that many of us lose heart on the spiritual journey because we're bored. Our spiritual practices – prayer, reading the Bible, saying an 'office' – have died on us. We're going through the motions and are secretly glad when we oversleep or have to catch the early train, which means we've missed the time we usually do these things. The counter argument of course is, 'How can God be boring?' This is the Creator of colour, the Maker of mountains, the Genius in Michelangelo, the Inventor of children's smiles, 'the Lord, the Giver of life'. But the truth is that sometimes we find the green field has turned grey, and prayer is simply a chore. We feel the failure of again being an absolute beginner who hasn't left first base.

Perhaps we can turn that very feeling around and claim the value of having a beginner's heart. A beginner's heart is prepared to learn. We're up for all the help we can get. We're prepared to try new things. We'll attempt a new path up the mountain. Sometimes indeed our boredom is the result of staying too long on the lower slopes. We need to try the higher ground. We've lost sight of God because he's gone on ahead and wants us to follow. God won't humour or patronize us. There are bigger and better things for us to grow into than to play in the sunny pastures all our lives. There are new routes to attempt, peaks to climb, risks to take; there's a bracing quality about the high ground. Certainly we could leave the mountains altogether and saunter back to town, but what a loss!

These new routes might take us into serious Bible study, taking a course and letting the stimulating winds of scholarship deepen our love of the Word. On the other hand fresh spiritual exploration might lead us to a silent prayer group where we take our first stumbling steps into contemplative prayer, lurching between delight in the new experience and panic at the sheer 'exposure' we feel walking along the edge of a spiritual precipice. Another person might go on retreat and discover the freedom of a few days of no responsibility except to be accountable before God. Another might explore the idea of having a spiritual director to talk to on a regular basis about the journey they are undertaking, risking the feelings of foolishness and discovering the release of being listened to and valued. Someone else might arrange to go to Iona or Taizé to feast on a different diet and experience the risks of community. Another person might tackle the world of icons and encounter the disorientating way an icon addresses the viewer by creating a focal point in front of the icon instead of behind it, so drawing the viewer into direct engagement with the Lord.

When I've had trouble keeping contact with God, I've known, at least intellectually, that it's not God's fault. God doesn't play hide and seek with us. I've therefore needed to consider where I should look to rejuvenate my journey. Usually what has been necessary has been some move out of my areas of sterile comfort and into new territory, higher ground. I remember when I was hanging loose as a diocesan youth chaplain how important it was that a monk challenged me to spend a solid time each day in silence. (He said half an hour but I've rarely managed that.) I remember how liberating it was when I discovered the place of the imagination in prayer and found that I could meet Jesus by the well (from John 4) and bring to meet him there the people I wanted him to make whole. I remember the first time I went to the Holy Land and being transfixed by Capernaum and the knowledge that Jesus had walked that very 50 yards from the synagogue to Peter's mother-in-law's house, and how these encounters revitalized my reading of the Gospels.

In other words, I think we have to be prepared to move on, to trek higher up the mountain, if we're getting stuck at base camp. Going back down the mountain or fretting at base camp won't usually bring the refreshment we need. It's much more likely that we need to make an intentional spiritual journey and tackle some of the ideas in the last two paragraphs, or go on a pilgrimage, try a labyrinth, use multi-sensory prayer or a hundred other possibilities. We need to change the spiritual geography and encounter the living Lord in a new place. 'He is God not of the dead, but of the living' (Matt. 22.32).

There are two background thoughts I want to put on the table at this point because I think they contribute to a lot of the problems people experience when they're needing to move on in their journey. The first is the reassurance that darkness isn't something to be feared. Indeed it's standard currency in the world of faith. It's not often that we grow spiritually through good times, when we're simply enjoying the sunlit uplands of faith and the eternal sunshine of God's love. My experience is that people grow when they have been in dark places, and that dark periods are good teachers because religious energy is actually in the dark questions themselves. If we recall the story of Jonah, he had to go inside the belly of the whale for a time before he could be turfed out unceremoniously on to a new shore. We can easily absorb society's obsession with success, total success and nothing but success, thereby taking a short cut from Palm Sunday to Easter Day (sadly taken by too many Christians in Holy Week anyway). Periods of loss and darkness, of doubt and despair, are likely to be part of any authentic Christian journey. We may not like to admit it, even to ourselves, but they form the black letters on the white sheet which, together, enable us to read what God is writing on our lives. It's part of growth. 'Fear not' (says the Bible, more times than anything else) – and afterwards, be thankful.

The other point to make is that spiritual growth is likely to move us beyond a simple splitting of people, doctrines and ethical positions into good and bad, right and wrong, friends and enemies, and towards a discovery that deep truth is often to be found in paradox. Governments, churches, the military, the media and the regulars down at the Dog and Duck probably prefer clear distinctions between true and false, the acceptable and the unacceptable, the in and the out. But life isn't like that. To take just one small example – me – I am a hopeless mixture of gold-dust and saw-dust. The fatal flaw goes right through me. Maturity will lead us to some sort of reckoning with paradox and the integration of opposites.

The priest and psychotherapist Beau Stevenson offers an interesting illustration:

How does a pilot land his or her plane safely just at the end of the runway, rather than overfly or land short of the runway? First of all the pilot lands at 3 degrees. On each side of the end of the runway there are lights with shutters calibrated for the plane landing at that angle. If the pilot sees two white lights, one on top of the other, the plane is coming in too high and will either overshoot the runway or will land too far down to stop safely at the end. If the pilot sees two red lights one on top of the other, the plane will land short of the runway, at Heathrow perhaps on the M25, which is not considered a good thing. If both white over red are seen together the landing will be safe, seeing the two extremes simultaneously. Jesus generally gives both the white and the red together as an expression of paradox: I believe they are meant to be seen simultaneously, rather than split into good and bad.

Stevenson goes on to give examples:

> 'My peace I give to you, not as the world gives you' (white
> light)
> 'If you follow me, be prepared to be crucified daily' (red
> light)

> 'Do you wish to save your life?' (white light)
> 'Then be prepared to lose it.' (red light)

> 'Families are the best of things [*sic*]' (white light)
> 'I come not to bring peace but a sword, a father against his
> son, a mother against her daughter, a daughter against
> her mother-in-law.' (red light)[3]

The New Testament is full of such apparent opposites. 'Whoever is not against us is for us' (Mark 9.40 – white light). But,
'Whoever is not with me is against me' (Matt. 12.30 – red
light). 'So the last will be first [white light], and the first
will be last [red light]' (Matt. 20.16). Paradox is therefore not
always something to resolve at all costs. It may be a way of
living with complexity and drawing more deeply on the wisdom
of the gospel and the grace of God, for God alone is equal to
our bewilderments and confusions. We are called, chiefly, to
hold the paradox in the 'liquid solution' of the Spirit. The
experience of paradox can in fact lead to a point of transformation where the complexity is raised to another level, often by
the use of symbol or sacrament. What seemed to be an impossible contradiction can become a point of new departure in
thinking and practice if we judge the moment well and intro-
duce a transforming image, symbol, story or sacrament. For
example, AIDS had been seen as the new leprosy, but when
Princess Diana was seen picking up and hugging an infected
child it became an iconic action which changed perceptions of
AIDS all over the world.

And that leads us into consideration not just of the individual
awakening of the sleeping giant of our spirituality, but of the

corporate dimension of that awakening which takes place in worship.

## Imagination and quality in worship

Against trends in churchgoing elsewhere, cathedrals are growing in popularity and the size of their congregations. They receive over 12 million visitors a year and you often hear of Christmas services being over-subscribed or repeated. Cathedrals and cathedral cities are 'destinations'. Sunday by Sunday, attendances are increasing. Why is this?

An obvious point is that cathedrals offer **a context of beauty** for worship. When I worked at Canterbury cathedral I could never go into the cathedral without my spirits being raised. During the day the soaring architecture made me walk on air; at night the dark shapes and shadows spoke of God's numinous mystery. I would take lively young people into the cathedral in complete darkness and then flick on the lights of that super-lative nave. All chatting would cease instantly; a *mysterium tremendum* would fall upon everyone. In a culture grown casual in showing deference, cathedrals speak of a God worth taking seriously.

Cathedrals also offer **worship of undeniable quality.** The music, the preaching, the choreography, the sound quality, the building, the total experience, is like no other. You may be a believer, a searcher or a sceptic but you can't deny the high standard of the worship on offer. In terms of 'consumer satisfac-tion' cathedrals hit the jackpot in a way most parish churches can't even hope to emulate. People often come out of cathedral worship glowing.

Cathedral worship also offers both **physical and mental space.** It tends not towards prescription but towards invitation. You can explore the world of faith without the danger of being asked to stand for churchwarden on your second visit. Physical spaciousness positively encourages personal reflection, brought on, perhaps, by the wonder of the building and the brush of angels' wings. People come for all sorts of reasons – the search for beauty and quality of worship, a desire to think about faith, escape from the machinations of the local church, habit, long family connection, support of a chorister son or daughter, being a visitor from abroad, and much more. The great thing is there's room for all.

Those coming to cathedral worship also know they will **encounter depth**. You never know in a local church whether you will arrive at a traditional Eucharist, a children's service, a pet service, or one that is simply alien in style, church tradition or taste in coffee. Some churches (not in the diocese of Oxford) can seem to infantilize their congregations in an attempt to be accessible and family-friendly. However, many thoughtful people are truly looking for a deeper engagement with the Christian faith. They have genuine questions, real inquisitiveness, and a desire to be taken seriously. By and large, cathedrals will meet those needs.

However, there is more to it than that. If we have lost the warmth and reality of our relationship with Christ the anonymity of a cathedral may mean it will only be a temporary resting place, not a final destination. The humble local church has much to offer if it can just get things right. That, however, is the crunch. Stuart Murray in his book *Post-Christendom* writes:

> Many Christians have left church, weary of its demands, irrelevance and self-absorption. Discussions with them highlight unfulfilled longings from their experience of church – encountering God in worship; authentic community; earthed spirituality; cultural relevance; and freedom to grow as human beings and followers of Jesus. This demanding but simple agenda means reinventing and re-imagining, rather than restructuring, church.[4]

If a church seems like an anxious parent trying to enforce minimum standards of behaviour from a diverse family, or an in-turned religious club arguing over its constitution, or a place that keeps people paddling interminably in the shallow end of faith, then it needs the full-blown gale of the Spirit to stir up the waters and remind them of what a church should be.

So if the sleeping giant of the church is to be awakened through the creativity of its worship and the life that flows out of it, what kind of things will it need to attend to? Living worship like that is going to be:

**Atmospheric.** When I went back to the ecumenical, international community at Taizé for the first time for many years, I arrived after a 24-hour drive through England and France in time for the Sunday morning Eucharist. I sat down in the midst of 5,000 young people sitting on the floor, waiting silently and expectantly for 80 white-clad monks to come in and kneel before the huge orange and yellow drapes and the hundreds of candles that formed a focus at one end of the church. Then the singing began, simple, melodic and haunting, and before I knew it, I was holding back the tears. It was an experience of such intensity and beauty that it touched my deepest desire for God. Although I knew nobody around me, I knew I was 'home'. This is what attention to the aesthetic context of worship can do, as well as its content (of which much more could be said about Taizé). Lighting, décor, symbols, silence and much more have a significant effect on the way we respond to worship. The church building at Taizé has all the refinement of an aircraft hangar, but it doesn't matter because the community has attended carefully to the atmosphere inside. The local church can help many searchers by attending to the question of atmosphere in its worship.

**Symbolic and sacramental.** Some years ago there was a huge landslide in Central America and many people were swept away and lost. The church building had not been damaged and the following Sunday it was packed as people brought their grief and bewilderment. The time came for the sermon. The priest went into the pulpit and said nothing. Then he reached down and picked up a large nail and a hammer. With loud blows he drove the nail ferociously into the pulpit and then, still without a word, he left the pulpit and went to kneel in front of the crucified Christ. The congregation knew what had been said. They too had been crucified as a village, but they would rise again. This is the power of a thoughtfully used symbol. When we are trying to get in touch with faith again it's often very important to avoid overusing words and concepts which can easily mislead or bruise people, but to use instead the silent voice of symbols and sacraments. Lighting a candle, holding a hand cross, gazing at an icon or a thought-provoking image on a screen, tasting bread and wine – these may be the supple silver strings that draw us back to God.

**Story-shaped.** The Christian faith has been story-shaped from the first. Transformation occurs when our own stories are brought into fruitful interaction with the story of God. It's the collision, fusion or conversation between these stories that makes for change. If personal stories are brought into church, worship comes alive. A young person's testimony may be the most vivid moment in a confirmation. Some churches interview a member of the congregation, perhaps once every two weeks or once a month, on what it's like being a Christian in their work or life context. The big question in society today is, as ever, 'How then shall we live?' The Christian answer lies in the lived experience of the people of God, and the penny of discipleship then begins to drop. But this experience is lived against the constant background of the story of Jesus which needs to be told and retold in word, drama, film, paint, dance, enacted parable – in every possible way. This is the story that has changed the world; it mustn't be the giant that we've allowed to fall asleep and can't wake up.

**Relational.** Our personal stories need to have integrity and it's the quality of our lives and relationships that makes the faith credible or not. A couple went to a church and said afterwards that the people were all very polite but it was like a family who had just had an argument. No one is likely to be drawn to faith, or back to faith, in a community like that. We often beat ourselves up by reminding each other of the oft-repeated observation on the early Church by a pagan author, 'See how these Christians love one another.' Nevertheless, nothing would probably contribute more to people finding faith today than that statement being true of the contemporary Church. And this reality is experienced, or not, in the heart of a church's life, which is its worship. It's there that people know whether it's all true. Good worship is not where we forget about each other because we are so focused on the glory of God, but where we see each other in a fresh way, as truly our brothers and sisters, because we are suffused by the glory of God.

**Liquid.** No one is quite sure what liquid worship means but the phrase feels as if it's telling us something important. For me, it's about worship that isn't set so solidly in text that it can't escape, worship that isn't so formalized that to cough in the wrong place is to invalidate it, and worship that isn't so self-conscious that it always seems to be looking in a mirror rather than towards God. If we are to find God again many of us will need worship that has a sense of naturalness and flow about it. Perhaps that's why many people appreciate worship particularly when it's taken out of our churches and placed in the open air, by a river or on a hillside. Like the rituals of any family, worship keeps its shape but it evolves. It isn't fixed and final. It's liquid.

**Christ-centred.** For worship to touch those parts of us that have gone into spiritual hibernation, it needs to focus on the Main Man. It's not sufficient for worship to be nicely numinous and languidly liquid. That way it might just end up vaguely vacuous. Jesus is the pivotal point of the Christian faith; he's what it's all about. And he's our trump card. So worship that hopes to engage the searcher and revive those whose faith is flagging is bound to reintroduce Christ as the touchstone, the person in whom divine lightning struck the earth, 'the pioneer and perfecter of our faith' (Heb. 12.2). How worship does this is the weekly task of tens of thousands of clergy and lay people. All we can ask is that those who lead worship never lose sight of that overarching principle – it's all about Jesus Christ.

It may be that we feel powerless at the end of this list of desirable qualities in worship because the churches we know don't demonstrate that imagination and quality, and we have no handle on changing things. The answer might lie in finding a church further afield or, even more positively, in offering to help in some of the ways mentioned both in this chapter and the next. Clergy are understandably protective of that which they hold most dear, so the offer needs to be made carefully, but I know that when I was a vicar I was delighted at the skills I found in the congregation when we set up a Worship Group to oversee the development of all aspects of worship in the church. Among them were teachers who knew about communication, musicians who were on the ball with all things musical, a handyman for the all-age service visual aids, a BBC sound engineer, even a soft-furnishings adviser! Ask, and it will be given you.

## Can the giant wake up?

I've wanted to suggest that in renewing our spiritual practice, both individually and corporately, the sleeping giant of our inner lives can be woken up. The giant can breathe deeply and live. I'm convinced, however, that this takes intentional effort. We can't simply stay in the icy water clinging to the wreckage of our previous way of praying and knowing God, believing that the ship will somehow miraculously reconstitute itself. I think two conversations are necessary; one is with a wise accompanier of our choice; the other is with God. Both conversations need space and time, for which I've said we need to slow down. And both need a commitment to try something new, to set off for the higher slopes. The evidence of many pilgrims is that the view from up there may still be wrapped in mist, but it can also be truly inspirational. A new expedition starts every day.

# 10

## *Communities of grace*

The writer A. N. Wilson announced his return to faith in a news-paper article at Easter 2009. He lost his faith in his thirties and began to rail against Christianity, writing a book on Jesus which made him out to be merely a failed messianic prophet. On his return he wrote:

> Like most educated people in Britain and Northern Europe I have grown up in a culture that is overwhelmingly secular and anti-religious. The universities, broadcasters and media generally are not merely non-religious, they are positively anti. To my shame I believe it was this that made me lose faith and heart in my youth. It felt so uncool to be religious. With the mentality of a child in the playground, I felt at some visceral level that being religious was unsexy, like having spots or wearing specs . . . For ten or fifteen of my middle years, I too was one of the mockers. But as time passed I found myself going back to church, although at first only as a fellow traveller with the believers, not as one who shared the faith that Jesus had truly risen from the grave. Some time over the last five or six years I found I had changed. When I took part in the [Palm Sunday] procession last week and heard the Gospel being chanted, I assented to it with complete simplicity. My own return to faith has surprised no one more than myself. Why did I return to it? Partially, perhaps, it is no more than the confidence I have gained with age . . . But there is more to it than that. *My belief has come about in*

*large measure because of the lives and examples of people
I have known – not the famous, not saints, but friends
and relations who have lived, and faced death, in the light
of the Resurrection story,* or in the quiet acceptance that
they have a future after they die.[1]

That's a fascinating story. It was the quiet lives of ordinary
Christians and the experience of a worshipping community
that brought Wilson back to faith. It might be like that for
others. Few things are more persuasive than the compassionate
embrace of a living community of Christ's disciples. Carl Jung
once told one of his patients, after six months of unsuccess-
ful therapy, that he thought he probably needed to find God.
'How do I find God, Dr Jung?' the man asked. 'I don't know,'
said Jung, 'but I suspect that if you find a group of people who
believe in God passionately and just spend time with them,
then you will find God.'

## The importance of community

We live in a society in which community is much sought and
rarely found. In the last 30 years there has been a sharp decline in
attendance at public meetings and membership of civic groups.
It's true that some groups have burgeoned, such as self-help
and therapeutic gatherings, and voluntary organizations have
multiplied, but these often tend to be either groups based on
personal need or groups that attract short-term commitment
but no long-term loyalty. The community groups that shape
society, either politically or socially, are waning. The Harvard
political scientist Robert Putnam called our current fragmented
style of living, 'bowling alone'.

And yet, says Jonathan Sacks,

Communities are a vital part of our social ecology. They
are where we gain our identity, preserve our traditions,
establish friendships and develop reciprocity ... They bridge

the gap between family and society. They are large enough to extend our sympathies but small enough to be intelligible. They are the human face of the common good, which would otherwise remain as an abstraction. They are where we learn to be citizens, carrying our share of the collective weight.

Sacks describes communities as 'workshops of virtue, not by what they teach but by what they are'.[2]

In a famous passage from the end of his book *After Virtue*, the philosopher Alastair MacIntyre raises the stakes even higher. He writes,

> What matters at this stage is the construction of local forms of community within which civility and intellectual and moral life can be sustained through the new dark ages which are already upon us . . . this time however the barbarians are not waiting beyond the frontiers. They have already been among us quite some time and it is our lack of consciousness of this that constitutes part of our predicament. We are waiting not for Godot but for another doubtless very different St. Benedict.[3]

Enter, the church.

## Churches as communities of grace

Pre-eminent among such communities in most localities are churches, those communities of grace which seek to be the human expression of divine love – fail as they must with such a high aspiration. I often meet people who have found a real home in their local church, often making chance contact with it through a baptism or funeral or the friendly presence of the vicar. These are the people, of course, who have found their local church to be a healthy community of faith and not the dysfunctional community that we considered in Chapter 2.

Some church life undeniably has a weak sense of community, a narrow attitude of enquiry, anaemic worship and a real disconnect from the issues that concern ordinary people. But most churches are much healthier than that.

When people lose touch with the living God one possible way back is for them to explore local churches to find a place that speaks their language and thinks with the same mental 'grammar' as they do, and has the same broad world-view. In a rural society with limited transport, people hoped this would be provided by the local church in the village. Today realism requires us to admit that consumer choice is bound to enter the decision-making process. What matters above all is the category I called 'world-view'. Without that, it may well be that randomly choosing a church is a crash waiting to happen. A church's world-view can be discerned in a variety of ways, ranging from academic anthropology to our own instinctive responses, but this world-view will be experienced in the style of worship, the kind of preaching, the way crises are handled, the way decisions are made, the way power is mediated. If you have been hurt before in a particular kind of church – whichever it may be – don't go there again! If a new church feels different and good, give it a try.

Above all, recognize that a church is not primarily an institution but a set of relationships. In the best-selling book *The Shack* the persons of the Trinity are depicted in wildly unconventional forms. Mack has come to a shack in the hills to try to deal with the terrible death of his daughter. In this piece he's in conversation with Jesus who's talking about the Church as if she's the woman he's in love with. Mack, finding no solace or help from his own church, says he's never met such a woman. Jesus says:

'Mack, that's because you're only seeing the institution, a man-made system. That's not what I came to build. What I see are people and their lives, a living breathing community of all those who love me, not buildings and programs.' Mack was a bit taken aback to hear Jesus talking about 'church' this way, but then again, it didn't really surprise him. It was a relief. 'So how do I become part of that church?' he asked. 'This woman you seem to be so gaga over.' 'It's simple, Mack. It's all about relationships and simply sharing life. What we are doing right now – just doing this – and being open and available to others around us. My church is all about people, and life is all about relationships. *You* can't build it. It's my job and I'm actually pretty good at it,' Jesus said with a chuckle.[4]

Of course church has to be more than this if it is to be a vehicle to carry the beliefs and values of a hugely divergent mass of people from one generation to another in particular social, historical and political contexts. However, the heart of that description is absolutely true. The local church is a community of people in relationship with each other, knowing that they have been blessed by God and now seek to be a blessing to others. If we have lost our way somewhere and God seems to have slipped off down a side street, perhaps we could look again for the local church that has our DNA, values its relationships, and above all, knows what it's for.

So what is that, precisely?

## Living Christ's life after him

I wonder if you would be happy if you found a church that really worked to the job description now accepted by large parts of the Church, known as the Five Marks of Mission? Those marks are:

- To proclaim the good news of the kingdom
- To teach, baptize and nurture new believers
- To respond to human need by loving service
- To seek to transform the unjust structures of society
- To strive to safeguard the integrity of creation, and sustain and renew the life of the earth.

If that was truly the goal of the local church wouldn't that be worth joining? It's a checklist to have at the top of every church council agenda. In essence what the church is called to do is to live Christ's life after him, to embody the vision, values and virtues of Jesus Christ. It's a high calling but that's what makes a healthy church so exciting. There's nothing mean and parochial about such an agenda; it's the stuff of dreams and the true goal of humanity.

But the person who has been bruised by the church and remains wary of re-engaging with it will point out that it's the style of operation as well as the goal that matters. So what factors of style will such a person look out for?

**Welcome:** The smile of God comes on a human face. Is this a place that will welcome me and be interested in who I am and what I bring? If I am only a 'new person' on a list to fit into pre-existing programmes then I might not be happy.

**Sanctuary:** I might need to be soaked in the grace of God after a week of being battered and evaluated by the latest performance indicators. Is this a place of nurture where I will be loved and valued, glued back together and sent out rejoicing?

**Simplicity:** In this over-complex world where I have somewhat lost my spiritual way, I may be looking for simple rhythms, such as the Celtic emphasis on heart, home and hub: cherishing *hearts* in the ways of the Spirit, offering *home* to friend and stranger, and being a *hub* that equips us all for effective discipleship through the week.

**Joy:** The abbot of Worth Abbey was travelling on the London Underground when a girl aged about 11 got into the carriage with her parents. She clearly had Down's Syndrome. She moved around the carriage tugging at people's sleeves and saying loudly, 'Are you happy? I'm happy. Are you happy?' No one was prepared to admit they were either happy or unhappy; many even ignored her. The abbot laughed, and she laughed and her parents laughed, but no one else seemed able to drop their masks. They were, after all, serious adults.[5] But what a sadness. We are made for joy. Jesus said to his disciples, 'I have said these things to you so that my joy may be in you, and that your joy may be complete' (John 15.11). Christ intends us for joy, the joy of the heavenly banquet about which he spoke so often. Does this local church I am considering joining have those intimations of joy?

**Playfulness:** I would even press the point one stage further. Does this church have an atmosphere of playfulness about it? Do people laugh at themselves (and not at others)? Is there a sense of the light-heartedness and playfulness that surely created this incredible world of crazy diversity and zany animals? Is this God's playground or just a group of people whose hobby is religion?

Again, you might be fearful that a church that combines these qualities with those characteristics of good worship listed in the last chapter simply doesn't exist. But the truth is that change can start with just one person, and if that person is hungry for God, so much the better. Our hunger for God may be just what a particular church needs because we bring disturbing questions that go beyond trite, conventional answers. We need reality. But reality doesn't lie in perfection. What we need in a community of grace is one that's on the way – trying, failing, having another go – but always motivated by the spirit of Jesus. That's the touchstone: do you recognize the spirit of Jesus? Is his the prevailing style? Would he feel at home?

### Find a church and hang around

The Westminster Confession famously states, 'The chief end of man is to glorify God and to enjoy him for ever.' Most Christians seem to think that we glorify God best through worship, and that to worship God means attending services of worship. The chief end of man therefore becomes going to church on a Sunday morning at ten o'clock. Something must have gone wrong with this logic. Michael Frost shows us where. In his book *Exiles* he writes:

> We glorify God in a number of ways: esteem, love, worship, service. In other words, when I feed the poor or share my food with a neighbour, I am glorifying God. When I study the Bible, I am glorifying God. When I take a prayer walk along a beach and give thanks to heaven for all its blessings, I am glorifying God. When I sit in the Impressionist Room at the Getty Center in Los Angeles and feel deep affection and admiration for the divine beauty in Van Gogh's irises, Monet's haystacks and Cezanne's apples, I am glorifying God. When I visit an orphanage in Vietnam, filled to overflowing with unwanted children dumped on the streets of Saigon, I am glorifying God. When I write to my government representatives demanding that they procure greater overseas aid, I am glorifying God. When I attend a gathering of fellow believers to sing or pray or undertake some other corporate worship activity, I am glorifying God. So although attending worship meetings is one of the ways we glorify God, it is not the only way.[6]

Nevertheless, Christians have always wanted to focus their glorifying of God by being together in the solidarity of God's family. And it's here that faith often rubs off. Barack Obama is one example among millions. After an agnostic upbringing with doses of atheism from a usually absent father, he became a Christian when he encountered the progressive potential of Christianity and Judaism in community organizing in South Chicago. He said it was the best education he ever had, based on a set of principles developed by a Jewish criminologist and an ex-Jesuit, with further material from Protestant theologians. Eventually, he wrote:

It was because of these newfound understandings – that religious commitment did not require me to suspend critical thinking, disengage with the battle for economic and social justice, or otherwise retreat from the world that I knew and loved – that I was finally able to walk down the aisle of Trinity United Church of Christ one day and be baptised. It came about as a choice and not an epiphany; the questions I had did not magically disappear. But kneeling beneath that cross on the South Side of Chicago, I felt God's spirit beckoning me, and I submitted myself to his will and dedicated myself to discovering his truth.[7]

Exposure to Christians and other people of faith left him wanting to discover the source of this powerful energy for change – which was, of course, the Spirit of God. The same can be true for someone wanting to rediscover the reality of God after the fire has diminished or gone out. One line of approach is to find a community of Christ's disciples and then just hang around and see what happens. A Jewish story illustrates the process well:

A man was going from village to village, everywhere asking the same question: 'Where can I find God?' Sometimes the rabbis would tell him to pray or to study and he did so, but he became more confused and God came no closer, so he moved on. One day he arrived in a little village in the middle of a huge forest and when he had found the rabbi he interrupted the rabbi's reading and asked his usual question, expecting one of the many conventional answers he always got. But the rabbi said, 'You've come to the right place, my child. God is in this village. Why don't you stay for a few days? You might meet him.' The man was puzzled, but he was also intrigued by the answer, so he stayed. For two or three days he wandered around the village asking people where God was that morning, but they would just smile and ask him to have a meal with them. Gradually he got to know the villagers and in time he began to help with their work. Every now and then he would see the rabbi and the rabbi would ask, 'Have you met God yet, my son?' and the man would smile, and sometimes he understood and sometimes he didn't. He stayed on in the village and the weeks stretched into months and eventually into years. He became part of the village and shared its life. He went with the men to the synagogue on Fridays and prayed with the rest of them, and sometimes he knew why he prayed and sometimes he didn't, and sometimes he said real prayers and sometimes he just said words. Then he would go home with one of the men for the Friday meal, and when they talked of God he was always assured that God was in the village, though the villager wasn't quite sure when or where he could be found. Gradually the young man began to believe that it was true, that God was in the village, though he wasn't quite sure where. He knew, however, that sometimes he had met him.

One day the rabbi came to him and said, 'You have met God now, my son, haven't you?' and the man said, 'Thank you, Rabbi, yes, I think I have. Though I'm not sure when, or how or where.' The rabbi replied, 'God isn't a person or a thing. You can't meet him that way. When you first came to our village you were so worried by your question that you couldn't recognize an answer when you heard it. Nor could you recognize God when you met him. Now you've stopped pressurizing and persecuting God you've found him, so now you can return to your home town if you wish.' So the man went back to his own town, and God went with him. And the man enjoyed studying and praying, and he knew that God was within himself and within other people. And other people knew it too, and sometimes they would ask him, 'Where can I find God?' And the man would answer, 'You have come to the right spot, my friend. God is in this place. Why don't you stay for a while? You might meet him.'

Or, as Carl Jung said, 'Find a group of people who believe in God passionately and just spend time with them; then you will find God.'

# 11

## *Friends reunited*

Bishop John V. Taylor once wrote, 'There are dark times when I can believe in God only because that man did, and I'd rather be deluded with him than right in any other company.'[1] You might have guessed that 'that man' is Jesus. Who would I trust on questions about the existence and love of God? Would it be the pundits of the chattering classes gathered round their Hampstead dining tables (nothing personal; my daughter lives there too) or would it be the One whose faultless life has inspired countless millions of people to live life at full stretch, to care for the poor and to love their impossible neighbour?

Jesus' trust in his Heavenly Father was the core belief of his life. Here was a man who seems to have been right about everything else – his teaching about human nature, about living well together, about the priority of love, about forgiveness, friendship, compassion and so on. Could he have been utterly misguided on the central belief and defining value of his life? I think not. Jesus was, in the right sense, obsessed by God. He was full of God, full of love. And when the world could stand his love no longer and hammered him on to a cross, he still went on loving.

It was, literally, a case of 'like Father, like Son'. Gerald Priestland, in a famous broadcast series called *The Case Against God*, put it like this: 'In Jesus, God was saying, "I am like this, and I am *so* like this that, as far as you are concerned, I *am* this."'[2] Nevertheless, as the author Mike Riddell puts it:

It's well said that no-one can see God and live. This isn't because anyone is going to punish you for prying. You're expected to poke and prod and lift the covers. But the fact is that none of us can handle a face-on session with the Source of all that is. Mere mortals get blown away by the intensity of God. To see God is to be consumed by God, and that's not to be, this side of the [big] river. So, like watching an eclipse of the sun, we have to have God filtered a little.[3]

Jesus is the filter.

It's strangely possible to go through many years of Christian faith and never really be confronted by the astonishing life at the heart of it. In my case, as a teenager I had many of the pieces of the Christian jigsaw from my upbringing, but the one vital missing piece was the central one around whom all the other pieces fitted. It was when I was shown the supreme significance of this life that I could metaphorically shout 'Eureka!' and start to fly in my Christian faith. This Jesus is the scandal at the heart of the faith. 'Who do you say that I am?' is the crucial question (Matt. 16.15). The answer I gave to that question changed my life completely.

If it might be the case that Jesus is as near as we can get to God's self-portrait, and what he said and did is the core of Christian belief, then he must be worth taking seriously, and what made him tick must be worth examining with the utmost respect. And if we then find, with John V. Taylor, that it might be worth believing in God because Jesus did, what would that mean?

## The One

If Jesus is the One who we think can really be trusted it might mean:

**Trusting as he trusted.** Jesus trusted in his Father even when he felt deserted. That harrowing cry from the cross, 'My God, my

God, why have you forsaken me?' (Mark 15.34) was a shout of protest by a son who knew his father was still there but was temporarily driven mad by his father staying out of sight at the key moment of his life. We might ourselves feel abandoned by the God we have trusted all our lives. Why has he melted away? Why has he drifted out of earshot when he's most needed? Jesus hung there between heaven and earth, and although he protested fiercely, he didn't stop trusting. Could we do the same?

**Praying as he prayed.** We might be finding prayer hollow and empty. Our prayers mock us as they return unopened and unread. Why bother? Answer: because Jesus prayed and that was the mainspring of his life. When asked, Jesus told his friends how he prayed, and came out with the consummate simplicity and comprehensiveness of the Lord's Prayer. If we can pray nothing else, could we trust Jesus on this one and use his prayer? The only extra I would suggest is that we say it deliberately and slowly, perhaps even pausing for a minute on a different clause every time we use it. That way it begins to sink in that there are some big issues at stake here.

**Worshipping as he worshipped.** Jesus remained a loyal – if radical – Jew all his life. As part of that commitment Jesus went to the synagogue on the Sabbath, no matter how frustrated he was with the ruling religious authorities. Does that ring a bell? It's good to keep going to church even when we're out of sorts with it. There's a lot of talk these days about hubs – electricity hubs, school hubs and so on. Churches are hubs of the spiritual energy that runs between the people of God. Hubs hold the network together and they focus the power. We may have been at the wrong hub but it's worth staying connected to the mains if the appliance is going to work.

**Living as he lived.** This sounds like setting our sights far too high, especially if we're feeling weak and floppy as a Christian.

Nevertheless, it's the experience of countless followers of this Jesus that if we try to keep in step with him and to live his life after him, somehow we find ourselves able to do it. Every post I've had in ministry I've felt out of my depth when I've set out ('This is where they finally rumble me'), and each time I've got into my stride as I've tried to follow my Leader – even if I've only been fooling myself!

The vital point here is surely this: if we make Jesus Christ our central value and commitment we can't go wrong. Even if, by some extraordinary miscalculation of the mind and heart, he was wrong about his Father, he nevertheless lived and taught a life that the world has acknowledged as possibly the best that a human life could be. That's not a bad model, whatever its philosophical grounding. It comes from having a centre that holds amid the slings and arrows of outrageous events. Fr Pedro Arrupe of the Society of Jesus said:

> What you are in love with, what seizes your imagination, will affect everything. It will decide what will get you out of bed in the morning, what you will do with your evening, how you spend your weekends, what you read, who you know, what breaks your heart, and what amazes you with joy and gratitude. Fall in love, stay in love, and it will decide everything.[4]

Or, to use some words of the historian Herbert Butterfield that I quote often, 'Hold fast to Christ, and for the rest be totally uncommitted.'[5]

## 'I call you friends'

The experience of losing touch with God must not be under-estimated. It's real, hard and devastating for anyone who has previously found faith liberating and life-giving. It can lead not only to play-acting and disillusion but in some extreme cases to bitterness and anger. However, we can't stay in that place without damaging ourselves and others. Although there's a well-trodden path into this dark forest, there's also a well-trodden path out of it. The philosopher Rabindranath Tagore wrote,

> I thought that my voyage had come to its end at the last limit of my power – the path before me was closed, that provisions were exhausted and the time come to take shelter in a silent obscurity. But I find that your will [O God] knows no end in me. And when old words die on the tongue, new melodies break forth from the heart; and where the old tracks are lost, new country is revealed with its wonders.[6]

One of the images used by Jesus to describe his relationship with his disciples, then and now, is that of friends. 'I do not call you servants any longer . . . but I have called you friends, because I have made known to you everything that I have heard from my Father' (John 15.15). And friendship, when broken, can emerge stronger than ever, with increased honesty and understanding, particularly when one side of the friendship never changed anyway. Christ never moves away from us. Remember, 'God doesn't know how to be absent.' Or as Paul says, 'Do you not realize that Jesus Christ is in you?' (2 Cor. 13.5). When we lose contact God doesn't sulk. We can't shake him off. And our return can then be sweet, as friends are reunited.

The distinguished novelist Maya Angelou was being interviewed for the magazine *Third Way* and remembered that she had a voice teacher when she was young who made her say 'God loves me.' She went on:

> That was in 1956, 46 years ago. I did it this morning. I sat on the side of the bed and the tears came and I said, 'I don't know why, but I know God loves me. I have not done anything to earn it and I've blown it four billion times and I am so grateful.' So grateful.[7]

Jesus said that he was calling us friends, and he's not fickle. Mind you, it's important that we don't think that that makes us the fickle ones either. People rarely walk away from Jesus out of spite. The reasons we looked at in the first section of the book are hopefully enough to demonstrate that the waning of faith and of the experience of God can have many roots and it doesn't help to blame ourselves. Faith is a mystery, not in an obscurantist sense, but in the sense that it's too rich for simple descriptions. Puzzles are there to be solved; mysteries are there to be explored. And why our faith waxes and wanes is ultimately a mystery rather than a puzzle.

However, when the desk is cleared and all our pencils are put away, there's one final and crucial issue to name. For many of us it's the key to returning to the bosom of the family.

## The Choice

Faith isn't a fluffy feeling that changes with the health of our bank balance and the state of our digestion. Faith is an attitude to life and as such it's something that we can choose, or not. We'll want to choose it on the best available evidence, of course, but ultimately no one can ever be forced to believe and surrender to God. There are no knock-down proofs, no guaranteed highs, no spiritual silver bullet. Whether we're coming to faith for the first time, or trying to find a lost path, we come to a point where we have to choose. Shall I suspend my disbelief and leap into space?

One of the basic questions we have to ask is the one Einstein asked at the end of his life. 'Now I see that the only question is, "Is the universe friendly?" ... I have begun to discover its physical meanings but the question that haunts me is, "Is it friendly?"' Richard Rohr, commenting on this, says:

> Is this whole thing out there on our side or not? Is the universe hostile or benevolent? Is it radically okay or is it not? The gift of true religion is that it parts the veil, returns

us to the garden and tells us our primal experience was trustworthy. It reassures us that we live in a benevolent universe, and it is on our side. The universe, it reassures us, is radical grace. Therefore, we do not need to be afraid. Scarcity is not the primary experience but abundance. Knowing this, we can relax and let go.[8]

Of course in one sense the universe is neutral towards us; it can be seen, validly and in scientific description, as immense and cold and unforgiving. But beyond its sheer physicality Rohr is reminding us that it's the creation of a Lover and not a cosmic joke. Do we choose to believe that? It's not provable but it's chooseable.

Here's a second way of putting the question. How do we best describe the reality we inhabit? Again, it's a choice. The secular vision tries to predominate in the West (although it's always being frustrated by new outbreaks of transcendence – whether UFOs, the paranormal, angels, visions, 'miracles' and so on). However, as Rohr says:

> After a while, secularism is boring. It's a dead-end vision; in a secular world the universe is not enchanted. The bush doesn't burn; it's just a shrub. [Western] culture wants to break out of secularism. Materialism doesn't name our reality adequately.[9]

People of faith believe that spiritual, metaphysical reality is, at the same time, both hidden and revealed in the physical world; there is a complete interpenetration of the two (which is why the sacramental view of life is so perceptive and accurate, talking of 'outward and visible signs of inward and spiritual grace'). Do we want to live within a closed secular world-view or an open spiritual one? The choice is ours.

Here's another version of the Choice. Do we see religion as one ideology competing with others for our acceptance and adoption, or as a way of seeing the world and everything in it? Many of us would maintain that true religion is not one of a thousand things but *the way we see* a thousand things. Faith is a process before it has content, and that process is about how we see. And not just how we see a particular range of things that are congenial to religion; it's how we see everything. The world says 'Seeing is believing,' but the Christian says 'Believing is seeing.' True believing will enable us to see well and to distinguish reality from fantasy.

So faith is not a thing in itself, although it has a huge treasure store for us to investigate later on. Rather, faith is like a window in a house which we value not so much for the thickness or quality of the glass as for what we can see through it. Our task – our choice – therefore is to keep the glass clean. A Christian is a window cleaner. Through the glass of faith we see everything as it truly is, sparkling in the sunlight or drenched in torrential rain. Faith doesn't have a sentimental, rosy view of reality; it's absolutely realistic, but it also sees everything as shot through with the presence of God, who is always active in sustaining or redeeming every bit of life. Our choice, then, is whether to subscribe to that way of looking at life or not. If we can dissociate faith from being simply one ideology among many, and understand it rather as a way of seeing all of life (and every ideology), then the choice is clear. Is this the glass, the lens, through which we want to look – 'or do we look for another?'

## *Beginning again*

When it comes to prayer most of us are beginners. Some of us are 'experienced beginners' because we've begun again in trying to pray so many times, having left the field in disarray so many times as well. But I find that rather encouraging. It would be more depressing if I felt there was a class of 'super Christians' who had prayer sorted, whereas, try as I might, I kept on failing. If there was a technique that guaranteed success we'd have found it by now. But there isn't, because prayer is a relationship rather than what you learn for an A level in Spirituality. To use the category of this chapter, prayer is a friendship.

Friendships are flexible and variable, and they're even more problematic when you can't see your friend and when you only hear your friend through a very distinctive use of the word 'hear'. So the friendship can break down, the lines go dead, we enter a silent land. And it feels like failure. The writer Samuel Beckett once said to an actor who despaired about his performance at a rehearsal, 'Never mind. Try again; fail again; but fail better.' As an experienced beginner I'd like to fail better at prayer each time I return to the stage.

Christopher Jamieson of Worth Abbey tells this story:

> A young monk once went to see his superior: 'Father,' he said, 'I must leave the monastery because I clearly don't have a vocation to be a monk.' When the older monk asked why, the younger monk replied, 'In spite of daily resolutions to be good-tempered, chaste and sober, I keep on sinning. So I feel I'm not suited to the monastic life.' The older monk looked at him with compassion and said, 'Brother, the monastic life is this: I rise up and I fall down, I rise up and I fall down, I rise up and I fall down.' The young monk stayed and persevered.[10]

In any case, prayer is more about God than it is about us. All we have to do is turn up and sit in the sun flowing from the presence of God. Prayer in that sense is like sunbathing. We don't have to do anything beyond being there, resting in God. For myself I like to believe the wisdom of my daughter who, when five years old and sitting at the tea table, and apropros of nothing at all, announced, 'God is like love going everywhere.' Augustine would have approved. If God seems distant there's no need to get tense and anxious. Perhaps we could simply go and sunbathe. The sun gets everywhere. (I mentioned a number of other approaches to prayer in Chapter 9.)

Let's return to an image from a previous chapter. Late in his life the spiritual writer Henri Nouwen became fascinated by trapeze artists. He was entranced by the idea of taking off into the void high above the crowd and flying unprotected through the air. When you have let go, he mused, there's nothing more you can do except trust – in particular, trust that the other acrobat will catch you. Everything depends on the catcher. What we have to do when we come near to faith, or when we're trying to be open to faith again, is to gather ourselves, breathe deeply, and leap into space, trusting in the One who catches everything. The One we're flying towards is none other than the One who calls us friends. His smile broadens as we come closer. All we have to do is reach out.

When we're flying through the void we'll feel both gloriously free and also very vulnerable. That's the nature of faith. Bear Grylls is a Christian well known for television programmes about his adventures in the wild. He uses the image of leaping as language that's common to both his career and his faith. 'When you're a kid,' he says, 'you never look before you leap. Now I know better – but I still leap.'[11] Following Christ is about making that leap. It gives us 'perfect freedom', and makes all of life wonderfully risky. Unfortunately the Christian faith has become associated for many people (especially teenagers) with avoiding risk, playing safe and preserving the status quo. The witness of Christians through the centuries, however, is that faith calls us out of safe ground and into liminal space, that is, space on the edge of the normal world of 'business as usual'. Liminal space is a threshold between old and new, where we're no longer trapped in safe conventions but open to change, to learn and to be transformed.

If we stop being interested in change then we've abandoned the pilgrimage of faith. God can only really do something new in us if we give up the safe boxes where we place our religious paraphernalia before climbing into the box and closing the lid. When we're out on the journey, or 'flying through the air', then God can deconstruct our normal world and open our minds to wonder. It's where we might re-find faith, re-find God. Friends reunited.

Everything depends on the Catcher, except for one thing.

We have to leap.

# *Notes*

## A word at the beginning

1 John Humphrys, *In God We Doubt* (London: Hodder and Stoughton, 2007), p. 36.
2 Andrew O'Hagan, *Be Near Me* (London: Faber and Faber, 2006), p. 88.

## 1 When the well runs dry

1 Henri Nouwen, *Sabbatical Journey* (New York: Crossroad, 1998).
2 Article in *Church Times*, 24/31 December 2010.
3 'The secret life of Mother Teresa', *Time*, 3 September 2007.

## 2 The Old Curiosity Shop

1 Richard Holloway, *Between the Monster and the Saint* (Edinburgh: Canongate, 2008), p. 126.
2 Letter to author quoted in Richard Harries, *God Outside the Box* (London: SPCK, 2002), p. 3.
3 John Saxbee, *No Faith in Religion* (Winchester: O Books, 2009), p. 1.
4 Anne Rice, Facebook, August 2010, quoted by Mitchell Landsberg, *Los Angeles Times*, 7 August 2010.
5 Alison Morgan, *The Wild Gospel* (Oxford: Monarch, 2004), p. 189.
6 Michael Frost, *Exiles* (Peabody, Mass.: Hendrickson, 2006), p. 124.
7 Victor Turner, *The Ritual Process* (Chicago: Aldine, 1969).
8 Greg Hawkins and Cally Parkinson, *Reveal* (Chicago: Willow Creek, 2007).
9 Richard Giles, *Creating Uncommon Worship* (Norwich: Canterbury Press, 2004), p. 22.
10 Diarmaid MacCulloch, *The Guardian*, 22 December 2009.
11 Alice Walker, *The Color Purple* (London: Phoenix, 2004), p. 174.

## 3 The tragic facts of life

1 Justine Picardie, *Times 2*, 1 May 2010.
2 Andrew Motion in Joan Bakewell (ed.), *Belief* (London: Duckworth, 2005), p. 223.

3 Fyodor Dostoevsky, *The Idiot* (many publishers).

4 John V. Taylor, source untraced.

5 Samantha Morton, *The Week*, 15 May 2010.

6 John Humphrys, *In God We Doubt* (London: Hodder and Stoughton, 2007), p. 34.

7 Emmanuel Levinas, 'Loving the Torah more than God' in *Difficult Freedom* (Baltimore: Johns Hopkins University Press, 1990).

## 4 The chattering culture

1 Friedrich Nietzsche, *The Gay Science* (New York: Vintage Books, 1974), p. 182.

2 Minette Marrin, *Sunday Times*, December 2002.

3 Jonathan Sacks, 'Religion in twenty-first century Britain', 2009 Annual Theos Lecture.

4 Richard Dawkins, *Unweaving the Rainbow* (London: Penguin, 1998).

5 Charles Saatchi, interview in *The Times*, 4 April 2010.

6 Friedrich Nietzsche, *Beyond Good and Evil* (New York: Vintage Books, 1989).

7 A. A. Gill, *Sunday Times*, June 2000.

8 Julian Barnes, *Nothing to be Frightened of* (London: Vintage Books, 2009), pp. 1, 118, 57.

9 Source untraced.

10 Dietrich Bonhoeffer, *Letters and Papers from Prison* (New York: Macmillan, 1967), p. 188.

11 Steven Weinberg, conference 'Beyond belief: religion, reason and survival', November 2006.

12 Peter Atkins in John Cornwell (ed.), *Nature's Imagination – The Frontiers of Scientific Vision* (Oxford: Oxford University Press, 1995), p. 132.

13 Richard Dawkins, *The God Delusion* (London: Bantam Press, 2006), p. 31.

14 Barnes, *Nothing to be Frightened of*, p. 70.

15 Paul Davies, widely quoted, e.g. Orthoprax website, 9 June 2010.

16 Zygmunt Bauman, *Globalisation: The Human Consequences* (London: Burns and Oates, 2005), p. 155.

17 Jonathan Sacks, *The Times*, 19 December 2009.

18 Joanne Harris, *Chocolat* (London: Black Swan, 1991).

19 Melvyn Bragg, *Remember Me* (London: Hodder and Stoughton, 2008), p. 156.

20 Howard Jacobson, University Sermon, Oxford, 13 June 2010.

21 Ian Hislop, *Independent on Sunday*, 11 April 1993.

22 Miguel de Unamuno, *Tragic Sense of Life* (Qontro Classic Books, 2010).
23 Fyodor Dostoevsky, *The Brothers Karamazov* (various publishers).
24 Ian Blair, sermon in Cambridge, summer 2010.

## 5 Surviving the darkness

1 Vaclav Havel, *Disturbing the Peace* (New York: Knopf, 1991), p. 181.

## 6 Re-imagining faith

1 Sara Miles, *Take This Bread* (New York: Ballantine Books, 2007), p. 58.
2 John Saxbee, *No Faith in Religion* (Winchester: O Books, 2009), p. 6.
3 Richard Rohr, *Things Hidden: Scripture as Spirituality* (Cincinnati: St Anthony Messenger Press, 2007), p. 59.
4 Saxbee, *No Faith in Religion*, p. 140.
5 Martin Laird, *Into the Silent Land* (London: DLT, 2006), p. 15.
6 Annie Dillard, *Pilgrim at Tinker Creek* (New York: HarperCollins, 1985).
7 Ian Markham, *Against Atheism* (Chichester: Wiley-Blackwell, 2010), p. 53.
8 Jeanette Winterson in Bel Mooney, *Devout Sceptics* (London: Hodder and Stoughton, 2003), p. 185.
9 St Augustine, *Confessions* (various publishers).
10 Michael Ramsey, source untraced.
11 Rohr, *Things Hidden*, p. 115.
12 'The secret life of Mother Teresa', *Time*, 3 September 2007.
13 Rowan Williams, 'The Good Man Jesus and the Scoundrel Christ', *The Guardian*, 3 April 2010.
14 Dietrich Bonhoeffer, *Meditating on the Word* (Cambridge, Mass.: Cowley Publications, 1986).
15 Peter Rollins, *How (Not) to Speak of God* (London: SPCK, 2006), p. 42.

## 7 'Earth's crammed with heaven'

1 Sybil Thorndike, source untraced.
2 Elizabeth Barrett Browning, *Aurora Leigh*, bk 7, 1.
3 G. K. Chesterton, letter to his fiancée Frances.

4 Gerard Manley Hopkins, 'God's grandeur', from *Poems* (Oxford: Oxford University Press, 1967).

5 *The Times*, 29 May 2010.

6 G. K. Chesterton, 'Ecclesiastes', from *The White Knight and Other Poems* (London: Grant Richards, 1900).

7 Annie Dillard, *Pilgrim at Tinker Creek* (New York: HarperCollins, 1985), p. 254.

8 William Blake, *The Letters*, 1799.

9 Barry Lopez, *About This Life-Journey* (London: Panther, 2001).

10 St Augustine, *De Civit. Dei*, Book XVI.

11 Michael Paul Gallagher, *Dive Deeper* (London: DLT, 2001), p. 4.

## 8 'Yes' as a way of life

1 Bel Mooney, *Devout Sceptics* (London: Hodder and Stoughton, 2003), p. 5.

2 Etty Hillesum, *An Interrupted Life: The Diary and Letters 1941–43* (London: Persephone Books, 1999), p. 355.

3 Interview on Channel 4.

4 John V. Taylor, *A Matter of Life and Death* (London: SCM Press, 1986), p. 18.

5 Peter Wilcox, 'Glory' in Sam Wells and Sarah Coakley (eds), *Praying for England* (London: Continuum, 2008), p. 45.

6 Mooney, *Devout Sceptics*, p. 5.

7 D. H. Lawrence, *Letters*, I, p. 519.

8 George Steiner, *Real Presences* (Chicago: University of Chicago Press, 1989), p. 3.

9 Ian Markham, *Against Atheism* (Chichester: Wiley-Blackwell, 2010), p. 62.

10 Sting, *Sunday Times*, 18 October 2009.

11 Taylor, *Life and Death*, p. 12.

## 9 Awakening the sleeping giant

1 Stephen Cottrell, *Do Nothing to Change Your Life* (London: Church House Publishing, 2007), p. 63.

2 Paul Walker, 'You don't need to be religious' in *Retreats 2010* (Amersham: Retreat Association), p. 20.

3 Beau Stephenson, 'Healing by paradox in the Christian tradition', paper given at the Royal College of Psychiatrists, April 2010.

4 Stuart Murray, *Post-Christendom* (Milton Keynes: Paternoster, 2004), p. 276.

## 10 Communities of grace

1 A. N. Wilson, *Daily Mail*, 4 April 2009 (my italics).
2 Jonathan Sacks, *Celebrating Life* (London: HarperCollins, 2000), pp. 140, 143.
3 Alastair MacIntyre, *After Virtue* (London: Duckworth, 1981), p. 263.
4 William P. Young, *The Shack* (London: Hodder and Stoughton, 2008), p. 178.
5 Christopher Jamison, *Finding Sanctuary* (London: Orion Books, 2007), p. 80.
6 Michael Frost, *Exiles* (Peabody, Mass.: Hendrickson, 2006), p. 280.
7 Barack Obama, *The Audacity of Hope* (Edinburgh: Canongate Books, 2007), p. 208.

## 11 Friends reunited

1 John V. Taylor, *The Easter God* (London: Continuum, 2003), p. 38.
2 Gerald Priestland, *The Case Against God* (London: Collins, 1984), p. 10.
3 Mike Riddell, *Godzone* (Oxford: Lion, 1992), p. 21.
4 Pedro Arrupe in Richard Rohr, *Everything Belongs* (New York: Crossroad, 2003), p. 122.
5 Herbert Butterfield, *Christianity and History* (London: Bell, 1949), final page.
6 Source untraced.
7 Maya Angelou, *Third Way*, 2009.
8 Richard Rohr, *Things Hidden: Scripture as Spirituality* (Cincinnati: St Anthony Messenger Press, 2007), p. 69.
9 Rohr, *Things Hidden*, p. 116.
10 Christopher Jamison, *Finding Sanctuary* (London: Orion Books, 2007), p. 172.
11 Bear Grylls, *Alpha News*, 2010.